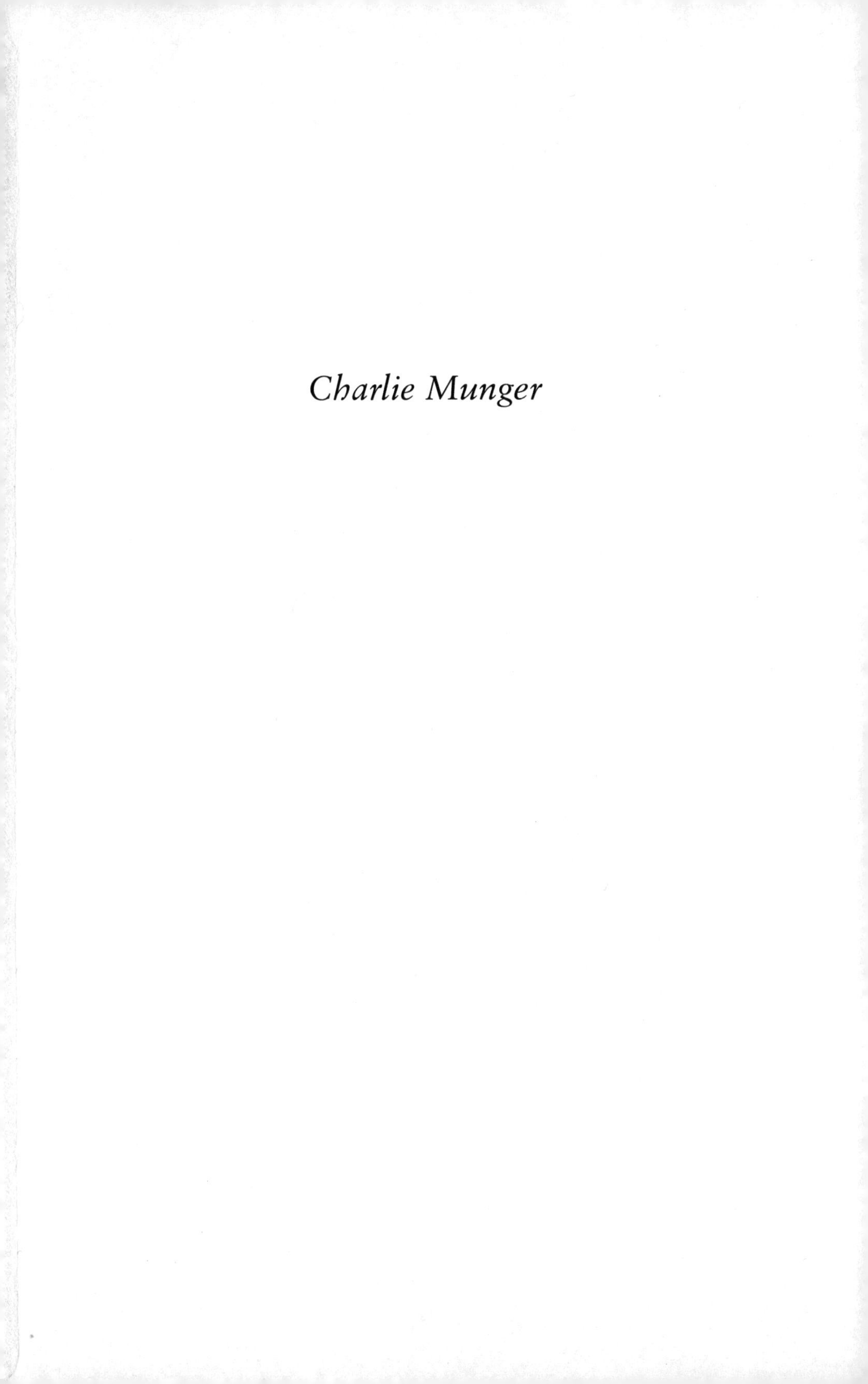

Charlie Munger

CHARLIE MUNGER

THE COMPLETE INVESTOR

TREN GRIFFIN

Columbia University Press
Publishers Since 1893

New York Chichester, West Sussex

Library of Congress Cataloging-in-Publication Data
Griffin, Trenholme J.
Charlie Munger: the complete investor / Tren Griffin.
pages cm
Includes bibliographical references and index.
ISBN 978-0-231-17098-7 (cloth : alk. paper); 978-0-231-54041-4 (ebook)
1. Munger, Charles T., 1924- 2. Investments. 3. Finance.
I. Munger, Charles T., 1924- II. Title.

HG172.M84G75 2015
332.6–dc23
2015002292

Columbia University Press books are printed on permanent
and durable acid-free paper.
This book is printed on paper with recycled content.
Printed in the United States of America

c 10 9 8 7 6 5 4 3 2 1

JACKET ILLUSTRATION:
Charlie Powell
COVER DESIGN:
Jordan Wannemacher

CONTENTS

Charlie Munger

INTRODUCTION

CHARLIE MUNGER IS one of the world's most successful investors and most interesting people. He is best known as the outspoken partner of Warren Buffett at the fabulously successful company known as Berkshire Hathaway. Buffett acknowledged Munger's contributions when he pointed out, "One plus one with Charlie and me certainly adds up to more than two."[1] Munger's success as an investor in businesses outside of Berkshire is also impressive. What is most interesting about Munger is not his success as an investor but the way he thinks and keeps his emotions under control.

Munger's ability to cut to the heart of an issue with a few well-chosen words is legendary, as is his desire to think independently. A fundamentally important truth about investing is that people rarely make decisions independently. This means that people who can think independently, gain control of their emotions, and avoid psychological errors have an advantage as investors. Buffett once illustrated Munger's desire to do his own thinking with this story:

> In 1985, a major investment banking house undertook to sell Scott Fetzer, offering it widely, but with no success. Upon reading of this strikeout, I wrote Ralph Schey, then and now Scott Fetzer's CEO, expressing an interest in buying the business. I had never met Ralph, but within a week we had a deal. Unfortunately, Scott Fetzer's letter of engagement with the banking firm provided it a 2.5 million dollar fee upon sale, even if it had nothing to do with finding the buyer. I guess the lead banker felt he should do something for his payment, so he graciously offered us a copy of the book on Scott Fetzer that his firm had prepared. With his customary tact, Charlie responded: I'll give you 2.5 million "not" to read it.
>
> —WARREN BUFFETT, CHAIRMAN'S LETTER, 1999

Stories like this one, together with colorful reports on what Munger has said in a range of settings, are a big part of what motivated me to write this book. Munger is such an interesting person, in no small part because he is, in a word, unrestrained. He says exactly what is on his mind, with little consideration given to tact and social conventions. This candor is valuable because sometimes we need to hear that the emperor is not wearing clothes. Munger has said that, although he has accumulated an outstanding record as a stock picker and accumulated substantial wealth, people should not emulate his example in life in general. He believes his life has been too devoted to improving his own mind and that peculiarities of his personality (including, but not limited to, irreverence) will make people unpopular if they blindly follow his example.

Munger recognizes that he is a lightning rod that may attract criticism on some issues. Munger said once, "I may be remembered as a wise ass," whereas his investing partner Warren Buffett will be remembered as a teacher. People sometimes say to me that they do not understand the fuss about Charlie Munger. Unfortunately, they are missing a key point: no one can ever be Charlie Munger, just like no one can be Warren Buffett. The point is not to treat anyone like a hero, but rather to consider whether Munger, like his idol Benjamin

Franklin, may have qualities, attributes, systems, or approaches to life that we might want to emulate, even in part. This same process explains why Munger has read hundreds of biographies. Learning from the success and failure of others is the fastest way to get smarter and wiser without a lot of pain.

Despite his irreverence, Munger is a teacher in his own inimitable way. He said once:

> The best thing a human being can do is help another human being know more.
>
> —CHARLIE MUNGER, BERKSHIRE ANNUAL MEETING, 2010

Much of what is interesting about Munger is explained by this simple sentence: "I observe what works and what doesn't and why." Life happens to Munger as it does to everyone, but unlike many people he thinks deeply about why things happen and works hard to learn from the experience.

Like Warren Buffett, Munger was born and raised in Omaha, Nebraska. He studied mathematics at the University of Michigan, but his path toward a college degree there was interrupted by World War II. During the war he served as a meteorologist in the U.S. military, receiving his training at the California Institute of Technology. After the war ended he was able to secure a place at Harvard Law School without an undergraduate degree. He learned to like California during his time at Cal Tech, and after law school he proceeded to form with a few partners what would become one of the nation's most prestigious law firms. Despite that success, he soon left the legal profession to invest on a full-time basis at the urging of Warren Buffett, whom he did not meet until after he was living in Pasadena, California. Between 1962 and 1975, Munger ran a partnership for a group of investors, which generated annual financial returns of nearly 20 percent, compared to a less than 5 percent return for the Dow Jones industrial average during the same period. Munger does not collect Ferraris or have a huge mansion. In many aspects of his life that do not involve ideas or investing, Munger is quite ordinary despite being a billionaire.

While Munger has delivered numerous speeches, written essays, and entertained legions of shareholders at Wesco Financial and Berkshire Hathaway annual meetings, his ideas have not yet been presented in a form that might be called a *unified theory*. This is probably because Munger's mind is capable of feats that are too hard for people of more conventional intelligence. For ordinary people, simultaneously juggling what he calls "multiple models" in their head is not an easy task without an understandable framework for the ideas. The intent of this book is to teach you how to think more like Charlie Munger.

How did I find my way to the ideas of Munger? The genesis of this book can be traced to the period immediately before the collapse of the Internet bubble. Many assumptions about investing were being questioned during this time. The wealth created during the Internet bubble was unreal to anyone paying attention. Marc Andreessen expressed it well when he said on Twitter that during this bubble, "the overwhelming feeling people had was panic—that they were missing out." What was going on seemed to be mass insanity, but most people thought to themselves, "What if it's real? What if value doubled or tripled again?" It was natural for anyone who, like me, was seeking answers about what was going on in the markets during this crazy period to read the views of successful and thoughtful investors.

To cope with what was going on in the markets, in the summer of 1999 I chartered a boat, hired a skipper, and told him to take my family to the San Juan Islands in Washington state. I took everything that had ever been written by and about Buffett with me on that trip. As I read Buffett's investing methods sitting on the deck of that boat, I found that it was actually Munger's ideas that resonated most with me. The specific question I most wanted answered at that time was how much of my stock in highly appreciated Internet and telecommunications companies I should sell. My family had a blast on the boat and the islands while I read and paced back and forth on the deck deep in thought. I did little else for a week but read and think; I was not a lot of fun on that trip. However, as the trip drew to a close, I had reached my conclusion: I would sell exactly half my Internet and telecom stocks. I decided that this would minimize regret, no matter what happened. It was not an optimal decision given the crash that followed, but I was happy with my decision then and remain so today. That trip was the start of my deep dive into value investing.

The value investing system developed by Ben Graham and used by Munger is the single best way for an ordinary investor to outperform a market index. While Graham value investing is a system, it is not possible for an investor following this approach to find success simply by following a set of rigid rules. The implementation of the Graham value investing system, the Berkshire system, or the systems of other value investors is an art, not a science. Value investing is not a connect-the-dots exercise. While fully understanding the Graham value investing system does not involve rocket science, most people will find that they either do not have the emotional and psychological control required or do not want to do the work necessary to outperform a market index. This is why Warren Buffett likes to say that "investing is simple, but not easy."[2] Munger's version of what Buffett said is: "Take a simple idea and take it seriously."

Much of this book is about how I have learned to better identify sources of emotional and psychological mistakes and what I learned from Munger about avoiding them. *Wall Street Journal* columnist Jason Zweig described one of the essential challenges in investing in an email to me:

> If it was easy to be like him and think like him, then there wouldn't be just one Charlie Munger. Turning oneself into a learning machine with multiple mental models . . . is very hard work, and the few people who succeed at doing it may still fail to benefit from it if they don't have the right temperament. This is why both Buffett and Munger keep going back to Graham: Being a true contrarian takes supreme courage and implacable calm. Buffett talks constantly about the

> "emotional framework" Graham provides; Charlie often says that most investors, no matter how smart, won't succeed because they have "the wrong temperament." I like to use a word from ancient Greek philosophy to describe this: *ataraxia*, or perfect imperturbability. You see it when Socrates goes on trial, when Nathan Hale is hanged, when Buffett invests in Goldman and when Charlie buys Wells Fargo the day before the bottom tick in March 2009.
>
> —JASON ZWEIG, EMAIL TO AUTHOR, OCTOBER 2014

To help myself better understand Munger's ideas and methods that relate specifically to investing, I created a framework composed of three elements: *principles, the right stuff*, and *variables*. This three-part framework is only one type of model that can be used to understand Munger's ideas and methods about investing. Other approaches to understanding Munger can be just as useful. My other intent in creating this framework was to create a checklist that can be used in investing. Munger is a strong proponent of a checklist approach to life's challenges:

> I'm a great believer in solving hard problems by using a checklist. You need to get all the likely and unlikely answers before you; otherwise it's easy to miss something important.
>
> —CHARLIE MUNGER, WESCO ANNUAL MEETING, 2007

Part of the benefit of creating a checklist is the process of writing down your ideas. I have always loved the point Buffett made about the importance of making the effort to actually put your ideas in writing. In Buffett's view, if you cannot write it down, you have not thought it through.

To best fulfill the promise of a book entitled *Charlie Munger: The Complete Investor*, it is essential to start out with a discussion of Graham value investing fundamentals because that will help convey an outline of where this book is going. The four fundamental principles of value investing as created by Ben Graham are as follows:

1. Treat a share of stock as a proportional ownership of the business.
2. Buy at a significant discount to intrinsic value to create a margin of safety.
3. Make a bipolar Mr. Market your servant rather than your master.
4. Be rational, objective, and dispassionate.

Munger has said these four bedrock Graham principles "will never be obsolete." An investor who does not follow these principles is not a Graham value investor. The Graham value investing system really is that simple.

Munger also believes the development and recognition of certain personal attributes are essential for a Graham value investor. These attributes represent "the right stuff" part of my framework. Munger believes that investors who can develop these attributes can train themselves to avoid common psychological and emotional mistakes and become successful investors. No one is ever going to be anything approaching perfect, but we can all get better over time. If we do not work constantly to improve these attributes, Munger believes, we can relapse into old mistakes and folly.

The final section of the book will discuss choices that a Graham value investor can make in establishing his or her own investing style and methodology. In other words, variations on the Graham value investing system can be created on top of the four fundamental value investing principles. No two Graham value investors are exactly alike in how their investing system is implemented. As just one example, Buffett has pointed out that while he and Munger are "Siamese twins, practically,"[3] they do have some differences in their approaches to investing.

The learning and teaching opportunities related to investing are essentially unlimited. Munger likes to say that a successful investor never stops being a "learning machine." This need to learn and relearn means that an investor must read and think constantly. Munger has said he does not know a single successful investor who does not read voraciously. His own children describe him as a "book with legs sticking out." Reading and learning will require some real work. There is a Zen saying that can be made applicable to this point: "In matters related to value investing, many people prefer chewing the menu to actually eating the food." I have learned not only to do the work but to love the work because it is intellectually satisfying. You can learn to at least enjoy the process—and maybe even love it too.

Before concluding this introduction, I should make a few points about the book itself. Its format is simple. Quotations from Munger have been set out in a logical order, typically followed by an explanation that I have written. Unless otherwise indicated, the quotation is something Munger has said. There is a glossary in the back of the book, so if you read a term you are not familiar with (e.g., *net present value*), you have a definition at hand.

The best way to teach people about how Munger thinks is to examine the dominant professional activity of his life in some depth. This book's focus is on how Munger thinks as an investor. Munger has called being a successful investor a "trained response." He believes that if you can learn to overcome behavior that drives poor decisions, you can gain an edge over other investors. Much of the context of the book will be about how Munger invests, but the discussion is just as applicable to making decisions in other aspects of life. By understanding the framework that supports Munger's ideas and methods, each of his individual public statements has even more meaning. For example, by learning about what he calls *worldly wisdom* and the *psychology of human misjudgment*, you can make better decisions. Learning about Munger's ideas and methods will forever change the way you think about investing and about life. You will make better decisions, be happier, and live a more fulfilling life.

I

THE BASICS OF THE GRAHAM VALUE INVESTING SYSTEM

LET'S GET STARTED with the most fundamental questions: what is the Graham value investing system, and who can benefit from it?

> [Ben Graham] was trying to invent a system anybody could use.
>
> —CHARLIE MUNGER, UNIVERSITY OF SOUTHERN CALIFORNIA (USC) BUSINESS SCHOOL, 1994

The critical point about Graham's system is that it is simple. Too many people take a situation and create complexity where none is needed. Take, for example, the old joke about unnecessary complexity at the National Aeronautics and Space Administration (NASA). The storyteller starts by saying that early in the space program NASA discovered that ballpoint pens would not work in zero gravity. NASA scientists spent a decade and huge amounts of money developing a pen that wrote not only in zero gravity but on almost any surface, at extremely low temperatures, and in any position of the astronaut. The punch line is: the Russians instead used a pencil. Graham value investing has the inherent simplicity of the pencil.

Munger believes that Ben Graham developed his value investing system to be relatively simple to understand and implement and thus valuable to an ordinary person. Graham value investing is not the only way to actively invest or speculate. For example, venture capital and private equity are very different approaches to investing from value investing, but Munger believes that these alternative *active* investing systems are not as accessible to the ordinary investor as Graham value investing is. So-called index-based (or passive) approaches to investing will be discussed shortly.

Warren Buffett says that investing is simple but not easy. When Graham value investors make mistakes, it is usually because they have done things that are hard for humans to avoid, like forgetting the inherent simplicity of the Graham value investing system, deviating from the fundamentals of the system, or making psychological or emotional mistakes related to implementation of the system.

Because investing is a probabilistic activity, decisions made in ways that are fundamentally sound may sometimes produce bad results. Sometimes a person will produce an unfavorable result even when his or her process is well constructed and executed. However, in the long run, it is always wise to focus on following the right process over any specific, intermediate outcome. Munger believes that when creating a successful investing process, complexity is not the investor's friend.

We have a passion for keeping things simple.

—CHARLIE MUNGER, WESCO ANNUAL MEETING, 2002

Peter Bevelin's book *Seeking Wisdom: From Darwin to Munger* has a section on the importance of simplicity. Bevelin advised: "Turn complicated problems into simple ones. Break down a problem into its components, but look at the problem holistically."[1] Keeping things as simple as possible, but no more so, is a constant theme in Munger's public statements. In a joint letter to shareholders, Munger and Buffett once wrote: "Simplicity has a way of improving performance through enabling us to better understand what we are doing."[2]

By focusing on finding decisions and bets that are easy, avoiding what is hard, and stripping away anything that is extraneous, Munger believes that an investor can make better decisions. By "tuning out folly" and swatting away unimportant things "so your mind isn't cluttered with them . . . you're better able to pick up a few sensible things to do," said Munger.[3] Focus enables both simplicity and clarity of thought, which in Munger's view leads to a more positive investing result.

> If something is too hard, we move on to something else. What could be simpler than that?
>
> —CHARLIE MUNGER, BERKSHIRE ANNUAL MEETING, 2006

> We have three baskets: in, out, and too tough. . . . We have to have a special insight, or we'll put it in the "too tough" basket.
>
> —CHARLIE MUNGER, WESCO ANNUAL MEETING, 2002

The Graham value investing system is designed to remove from the process any decisions that may lead an investor to make mistakes. The "yes" basket is tiny compared to the other two baskets because an investing decision that results in a "yes" will happen rarely.

Not all companies can be accurately valued using a Graham value investing process. It is perfectly natural for a person who follows the Graham system to acknowledge that fact and move on to other easy decisions. It is often disorienting to some people that a Graham value investor would admit to not knowing how to accurately value a company. Munger made this point with an analogy:

> Confucius said that real knowledge is knowing the extent of one's ignorance. Aristotle and Socrates said the same thing. Is it a skill that can be taught or learned? It probably can, if you have enough of a stake riding on the outcome. Some people are extraordinarily good at knowing the limits of their knowledge, because they have to be. Think of somebody who's been a professional

> tightrope walker for 20 years—and has survived. He couldn't survive as a tightrope walker for 20 years unless he knows exactly what he knows and what he doesn't know. He's worked so hard at it, because he knows if he gets it wrong he won't survive. The survivors know.
>
> —CHARLIE MUNGER, JASON ZWEIG INTERVIEW, 2014

Graham value investing is not about showboating or flouting one's intelligence. Instead, it is about doing things that are not likely to result in a mistake.

The successful Graham value investor also works diligently to reduce the downside risk of any investment. For this reason, the Graham value investing system tends to shine most brightly during a flat or falling stock market. The Graham value investing system is intentionally designed to underperform an index in a bull market; this is confusing to many people. The underperformance of the Graham value investing system during a bull market is an essential part of this style of investing. By giving up some of the upside in a bull market, the Graham value investor is able to outperform when the market is flat or down. Consider what Seth Klarman wrote in *Margin of Safety*: "Most investors are primarily oriented toward return, how much they can make and pay little attention to risk, how much they can lose."[4] He added, "The payoff from a risk-averse, long-term orientation is—just that—long term."[5]

Here is a story to further illustrate this point. An investor was walking in a park one day when she saw a frog sitting on a log at the edge of a pond. The frog looked right at her and said, "Excuse me, would you happen to be an investor?"

The investor replied, "Yes, I am. Why do you ask?"

"Well," replied the frog, "I am a stock speculator. My best client did not like my investing results so he put a spell on me and now I am a frog. The spell can be broken if an investor will kiss me."

The investor immediately reached over and picked up the frog, put him in her purse, and then started to walk home. The frog was concerned that he was not receiving a kiss and asked, "What are you doing? When do I get my kiss?"

The investor replied, "I'm not kissing you ever. You're worth a lot more to me as a talking frog than as a stock speculator."

If you cannot accept investing underperformance in the short term in order to achieve long-term investment outperformance, then you are not a candidate for Graham value investing. This is not a tragedy, since the Graham value investing system is not the only way to invest successfully. It is important to note that the goal of the Graham value investor is superior absolute performance, not just relative performance. An investor cannot spend the output of relative performance, only actual performance.

Failing conventionally is not the goal of the Graham value investor. Munger's approach is to invert the methods of most people:

> It's remarkable how much long-term advantage people like us have gotten by trying to be consistently not stupid, instead of trying to be very intelligent. There must be some wisdom in the folk saying, "It's the strong swimmers who drown."
>
> —CHARLIE MUNGER, WESCO ANNUAL REPORT, 1989

> What's the flip side, what can go wrong that I haven't seen?
>
> —CHARLIE MUNGER, *FORBES*, 1969

Munger's inclination to invert the usual approach to solving a problem is clearly evident when it comes to investing. In his view, investors will do better financially simply by being less stupid. One core idea Munger has borrowed from algebra is that many problems are best addressed backward. For example, by avoiding stupidity, a person can often discover what he or she wants through subtraction. By eliminating the stupid paths that one can take in life, a person can find the best way forward, even given inevitable risk, uncertainty, and ignorance. Not only does one often know a lot more about what is wrong than what is right, but disproving something may also require only one observation. In short, Munger's view is that being smart is often best achieved by not being stupid. Once, in an interview with Jason Zweig, Munger said it simply: "Knowing what you don't know is more useful than being brilliant."

Munger strives to find investments for which a significantly positive outcome is obvious. Because this type of investment is identified only rarely, Munger suggests that one be very patient but also very ready to aggressively invest when the time is right. To use a baseball analogy, Munger knows there are no called strikes in investing, so there is no need to swing at every pitch. When you find an obvious bet with a big upside, Munger's advice is simple: bet big!

> All the equity investors, in total, will surely bear a performance disadvantage per annum equal to the total croupiers' costs they have jointly elected to bear. This is an inescapable fact of life. And it is also inescapable that exactly half of the investors will get a result below the median result after the croupiers' take, which median result may well be somewhere between unexciting and lousy.
>
> —CHARLIE MUNGER, *PHILANTHROPY*, APRIL 1999

The point Munger makes immediately above about investing as a less-than-zero sum game after fees and expenses is mathematically irrefutable. John Bogle, the founder of the nonprofit mutual fund provider Vanguard, is perhaps the most successful person to ever evangelize this simple idea. Bogle wrote, "In many areas of the market, there will be a loser for every winner, so, on average, investors will get the return of that market less fees."[6] Columbia Business School professor, investor, and author Bruce Greenwald had his own take on this point, which I find compelling:

> Only in Woebegone can people out-invest the market. The average performance of all investors has to be the average performance of all assets. It's a zero-sum game if you judge it relative to the

> market. There are two sides to every trade. The best way to think about it is that every time you buy a stock, someone is selling . . . So you always have to ask the question, "Why am I on the right side of this trade?"
>
> —BRUCE GREENWALD, *BETTERMENT* INTERVIEW, 2013

Graham value investing would not work if markets were perfectly efficient. For this reason, the market's folly is the fundamental source of the Graham value investor's opportunity.

Munger's take on why investing is hard is simple:

> The idea that everyone can have wonderful results from stocks is inherently crazy. Nobody expects everyone to succeed at poker.
>
> —CHARLIE MUNGER, *DAILY JOURNAL* MEETING, 2013

> If [investing] weren't a little difficult, everybody would be rich.
>
> —CHARLIE MUNGER, *DAMN RIGHT*, 2000

> For a security to be mispriced, someone else must be a damn fool. It may be bad for the world, but not bad for Berkshire.
>
> —CHARLIE MUNGER, WESCO ANNUAL MEETING, 2008

Because the degree to which investors may collectively act like "damn fools" varies over time, opportunities to generate investment gains will inevitably arrive in a lumpy fashion. Successful Graham value investors spend most of their time reading and thinking, waiting for significant folly to inevitably raise its head. Although Graham value investors are bullish about the market in the long term, they do not make investing decisions based on short-term predictions about stocks or markets. When confronted with this idea, people will often ask, "Do you mean Graham value investors wait for mispriced assets to appear rather than predict the future in the short term?" The answer is an emphatic yes! The Graham value investor's job is to recognize mispriced assets when he or she sees them. This approach is hard for many people to accept.

At the core of the system is the idea that the investor must let go of his or her desire to make short-term predictions about the future. Some people just can't do that. Klarman wrote:

> The value discipline seems simple enough but is apparently a difficult one for most investors to grasp or adhere to. As Buffett has often observed, value investing is not a concept that can be learned and applied gradually over time. It is either absorbed or adopted at once, or it is never truly learned.
>
> —SETH KLARMAN, *MARGIN OF SAFETY*, 1991

As will be explained, the time of greatest activity for a Graham value investor is when the people who make up the market are fearful as evidenced by mispriced assets available for purchase. It is ironically because of downturns in markets that the Graham value investor finds his or her greatest source of profits.

Munger pointed this out:

> Most people who try [investing] don't do well at it. But the trouble is that if even 90 percent are no good, everyone looks around and says, "I'm the 10 percent."
>
> —CHARLIE MUNGER, WESCO ANNUAL MEETING, 2004

This aspect of human nature can be a troubling fact for a financial planner. Is it dangerous to tell a client that beating the market is possible even if you know that there is little chance that this person will actually do so? It may not be dangerous in and of itself, but it certainly creates substantial risk. The following is common yet perfectly good advice about investing and is true in most cases:

> It's not possible for investors to consistently outperform the market. Therefore you're best served investing in a diversified portfolio of low-cost index funds [or exchange-traded funds].

Although this advice is mostly true, it is provably false in the case of investors like Charlie Munger, Warren Buffett, Seth Klarman, Howard Marks, Bill Ruane, and other Graham value investors. Munger once said, "The top 3 or 4 percent of the investment management world will do fine."[7] The fact that Munger has outperformed the market does not necessarily mean that you can; however, it does mean that it is possible for some people to accomplish. Munger said the following about the Graham value investing system:

> It's a very simple set of ideas and the reason that our ideas have not spread faster is they're too simple. The professional classes can't justify their existence if that's all they have to say.
>
> —CHARLIE MUNGER, BBC INTERVIEW, 2009

Successfully learning and especially implementing the Graham value investing system is what Munger has called "a trained response." You must learn to overcome certain behavior that drives poor decisions. If you can do that successfully, Munger believes you can create an investing edge over other investors. Part of that trained response is to avoid distracting noise made by people who do not understand investing or who have a financial interest in keeping you from understanding investing. The task is made vastly harder by people who generate their income by making the investing process overly complex and harvesting their living from the psychological and emotional dysfunctions of investors. Munger told a story about the incentives of investment managers that is instructive:

> I think the reason why we got into such idiocy in investment management is best illustrated by a story that I tell about the guy who sold fishing tackle. I asked him, "My God, they're purple and green. Do fish really take these lures?" And he said, "Mister, I don't sell to fish."
>
> —CHARLIE MUNGER, USC BUSINESS SCHOOL, 1994

It can be hard for some people to make a living selling you something that is simple, but it is the best approach for the investor. Fortunately, the function of financial planning is being separated from the process of managing money. A financial planner provides the greatest value for clients simply by helping investors keep their emotional and psychological dysfunctions under control. If this behavior modification is effective, the financial planner will employ a range of techniques to help you not be your own worst enemy. In some cases, intense competition has started to reduce fees and increase transparency in financial planning and money management businesses. This competition has caused many financial planners to focus on more valuable services for customers, such as retirement and estate planning; some fees for money managers have come down as well.

Munger's advice is simple for people who decide that they should not try to outperform markets:

> Our standard prescription for the know-nothing investor with a long-term time horizon is a no-load index fund.
>
> —CHARLIE MUNGER, *KIPLINGER* INTERVIEW, 2005

Who is a "know-nothing" investor? The answer is simple for Munger: a know-nothing investor is someone who does not understand fundamentals of investing. Here is a simple suggestion from Seth Klarman for no-nothing investors: "If you can't beat the market, be the market."[8]

Buffett agreed: "By periodically investing in an index fund, for example, the know-nothing investor can actually outperform most investment professionals. Paradoxically, when 'dumb' money acknowledges its limitations, it ceases to be dumb."[9] What Buffett was talking about is the question of whether a person should be an active or a passive investor—concepts he learned from Benjamin Graham.

Passive investors are not completely passive because they still have choices to make. For example, passive investors must make asset allocation decisions (i.e., which types of investments to make) and determine what types of indexes to use within those asset classes. When making these choices, investors can still make emotional and psychological errors.

Even though passive investors must make some decisions, they are called passive because they do not make as many decisions as active investors. A better approach is perhaps to call these passive investors *index investors*. If a person is investing in a diversified portfolio of index funds and exchange-traded funds (ETFs), then he is an index investor. If a person is picking individual stocks and other securities, then she is an active investor. Many people engage in a mix of active and index investing. For example, some index funds are tweaked and include some choices about factors that can improve their performance. This factor style of index investing is discussed in the last section of this book: Value Investing vs. Factor Investing.

Being an active investor and somehow outperforming the market after fees and expenses may sound good to you. However, being a successful active investor requires massive amounts of time and work, plus the right emotional temperament. If you do not enjoy it, why do it? William Bernstein wrote:

> Successful investors . . . must possess an interest in the process. It's no different from carpentry, gardening, or parenting. If money management is not enjoyable, then a lousy job inevitably results, and, unfortunately, most people enjoy finance about as much as they do root canal work.
>
> —WILLIAM BERNSTEIN, *THE INVESTOR'S MANIFESTO*, 2012

In any event, investors must still make several key investing decisions, and understanding the ideas and methods of Munger will help them do so more successfully. Columbia Business School professor Bruce Greenwald summed up the challenge as follows: "Emotions are absolutely your enemy. You want to be a certain kind of mutant who is just completely different in their orientation to what's an attractive investment for the rest of the market."[10] Can you be the mutant that Professor Greenwald described?

As you read this book, think about whether you have the right stuff required to be a successful Graham value investor like Munger. Can you understand and implement the principles to make the required choices about value investing variables? It may well be that you find the whole investment process too boring to do it well enough to beat the market. You may conclude that you're too easily distracted, are likely to panic at the wrong time, or will too often follow the crowd into poorly performing investments. If you cannot be an effective Graham value investor or don't want to put in the effort required to do so, invest in a diversified portfolio of low-cost index funds and ETFs.

Some investors knowingly do a small amount of active investing for fun, much as they might gamble in Las Vegas. This can be logical as long as people remember that gambling is, well, gambling. Knowing the difference between gambling and investing is important. Investing is an action that defers consumption in the present in the hope that you will be able to consume more in the future. An investor has an expectation of a positive real rate of return, even though it is possible that this will not happen (especially in the short term). In other words, an investment is a net present value–positive activity (the likelihood of the net present value of the potential benefits minus the likelihood net present value of the potential losses is positive). Gambling is a form of present-moment consumption, and the net present long-term value of the activity is negative. Many people who think they are investing are actually gambling.

Some people try to outperform the market by saying essentially, "I can be smart about picking other people who will outperform the market via active investing." Munger believes that if something related to active investing is worth doing, then it is worth doing yourself. Munger has said on this point:

> I think you'll at least make fewer mistakes than people who think they can do anything, no matter how complex, by just hiring

somebody with a credible label. You don't have to hire out your thinking if you keep it simple.

—CHARLIE MUNGER, BERKSHIRE ANNUAL MEETING, 1994

What Munger meant is that outsourcing active investing to others, such as investment managers and brokers, is harder than doing it yourself. One way of doing it yourself is by buying a diversified portfolio or index funds/ETFs. Unfortunately, this approach is not enough to achieve financial success because investors must still make important investment choices; they will too often "chase performance" by buying into funds/ETFs when the market is high and selling when the market is low. If index investors did not need to make some choices, there would not be a behavior gap of approximately 2 percent between investors and the investing funds they buy. In other words, even if you choose to be an index investor and buy a low-cost portfolio of funds/ETFs, you still need to develop the trained response that will enable you to overcome the behavioral biases that can lead to making mistakes. What Munger teaches about investing is applicable in its own way to index investors. The ideas and methods described in this book are still very important for an index investor.

2

THE PRINCIPLES OF THE GRAHAM VALUE INVESTING SYSTEM

The number one idea is to view a stock as an ownership of the business.

—CHARLIE MUNGER, *HARVARD LAW BULLETIN*, 2001

Understanding how to be a good investor makes you a better business manager and vice versa.

—CHARLIE MUNGER, *KIPLINGER*, 2005

First Principle: Treat a Share of Stock as a Proportional Ownership of a Business

THIS FIRST PRINCIPLE of the Graham value investing system is the foundation on which any valuation must begin. Put simply: if you do not understand the actual business of the company, you cannot understand the value of assets related to that business, like a share of stock or a bond. Graham value investors approach any valuation as if they were actually buying a business in a private transaction.

In buying a business, Munger believes the place to start is at the bottom, with business fundamentals, and work up. What does the company sell and who are its customers and competitors? What are the key numbers that represent the value the business generates? The list of important questions that an investor must answer is extensive. For a true Graham value investor, there is no substitute for a bottom-up valuation process. In undertaking this process, Graham value investors are focused on the present value of the cash that will flow from the business during its lifetime and whether the business generates high, sustained, and consistent returns on capital. Many supplemental variations on this process exist, but the fundamental core of the valuation process is the same for all Graham value investors.

Effective Graham value investors are like great detectives. They are constantly looking for bottom-up clues about what has happened in the past and, more importantly, what is happening now. Graham value investors like Munger stay away from making predictions about how cash flows will change in the future based on projections and forecasts. What Munger looks for is a business that has a significant track record of generating high, sustained, and consistent financial returns. If valuing the business requires understanding how cash flows will change in the future based on factors like rapid technological change, Munger puts that business in the *too hard* pile and moves on to value other companies. Munger makes it quite clear that he does not have a way to value all companies, which is fine with him because he feels no need to do so. There are more than enough businesses that Munger can value using his valuation method to make him happy as an investor.

The key to understanding this first principle is understanding that Munger believes that a share of stock cannot be divorced from the fundamentals of the specific business. Munger's response to people who doubt his approach can be phrased as a question: if a share of stock is not a partial stake in a business, what exactly is it? Jason Zweig of the *Wall Street Journal,* who is a hero to Graham value investors, wrote that "a stock is not just a ticker symbol or an electronic blip; it's an ownership interest in an actual business, with an underlying value that does not depend on its share price."[1] For a Graham value investor, a share of IBM stock is just a small share of IBM's overall business. Munger believes that treating shares of a company as if they should be valued like baseball cards is a loser's game because it requires that you predict the behavior of often irrational and emotional herds of human beings. A Graham value investor puts short-term predictions about mass psychology in the *too hard* pile and focuses on what he or she can do successfully with far greater ease. Graham value investors do not spend time with top-down factors like monetary policy, consumer confidence, durable goods orders, and market sentiment in doing a business valuation or investing.

> Be motivated when you're buying and selling securities by reference to intrinsic value instead of price momentum.
>
> —CHARLIE MUNGER, *DAMN RIGHT*, 2000

As Ben Graham once pointed out, "It's an almost unbelievable fact that Wall Street never asks: how much is *the business* selling for?"[2]

That a famous Graham value investor like Munger or Buffett may make a statement about current economic conditions or market indicators does not mean that they purchase stocks based on that view or that they think they can make successful predictions about what the macroeconomy might do in the short term. Famous Graham value investors may also make positive statements in the press and at conferences about the future state of the economy in the long term. However, that does not mean they make investments based on those forecasts. There is a huge difference between what is interesting to learn about and what is useful in making an investment decision. For example, both Munger and Buffett are famously bullish on the U.S. economy in the long term, but that does not mean they make short-term predictions about the economy or incorporate them into investment decision making.

Munger is adamant about many points, including this core belief: you must value the business in order to value the stock. Graham value investors price assets based on their value to a private investor now (based on data from the present and past) rather than making predictions about markets in the future. If you focus on the value of the business, you have no need to predict short-term changes in the economy because that takes care of itself. When stocks are a bargain, people are fearful; when stocks are expensive, people are greedy.

> Crowd folly, the tendency of humans, under some circumstances, to resemble lemmings, explains much foolish thinking of brilliant men and much foolish behavior.
>
> —CHARLIE MUNGER, *PHILANTHROPY* ROUNDTABLE, 2000

If you do not follow the business to value the stock approach, in the view of Graham value investors, you are a *speculator* and not an *investor.* If you are an investor, you are trying to understand the value of the asset. By contrast, a speculator is trying to guess the price of the asset by predicting the behavior of others in the future. In other words, a speculator's objective is to make predictions about the psychology of large masses of people, which if you are both smart and experienced is a sobering thought. How good are you at predicting what people will do once assembled into a mob? The big danger related to this tendency is that you just end up following the crowd and doing what Munger talked about here:

> Mimicking the herd invites regression to the mean (merely average performance).
>
> —CHARLIE MUNGER, *POOR CHARLIE'S ALMANACK*, 2005

When speculators spend their time trying to guess what other speculators are trying to guess, the process quickly becomes both circular and absurd. Graham value investors do not treat a share of stock or a bond as a piece of paper to be traded back and forth. They also do not spend any time looking at technical charts of stock price movements, searching for things like *double bottoms* or

Hindenburg omens. The financial performance of speculators is, in a word, dismal, especially after fees, costs, and taxes. Even when speculators are right, it is almost inevitable that they are correct only once in a while. Too often, investors confuse luck with skill.

Munger is a firm believer in the Ben Graham view that "an investment operation is one which, upon thorough analysis, promises safety of principal and an adequate return. Operations not meeting these requirements are speculative."[3] Buffett has his own version:

> If you're an investor, you're looking on what the asset is going to do; if you're a speculator, you're commonly focusing on what the price of the object is going to do, and that's not our game.
>
> —WARREN BUFFETT, *OUTSTANDING INVESTOR DIGEST*, 1997

If you always bet with the crowd, you cannot beat the market—especially after fees, costs, and taxes. To outperform the market, sometimes you must be a contrarian, and you must be right on enough of those occasions when you're a contrarian.

For example, people who day-trade stocks using charts of past prices and other voodoo-like practices are speculators. You will hear them talk about how the market behaves rather than what the value of a given stock may be. A guess about market behavior based on a chart is just that—a guess! Speculators are focused on price, whether it may be an old baseball card or a share of stock. Graham value investors have a very different view than speculators. Seth Klarman wrote that "technical analysis is based on the presumption that past share price meanderings, rather than underlying business value, hold the key to future stock prices."[4]

Buffet used a story to illustrate the dangers of herd behavior in one of his Chairman's letters:

> Ben Graham told a story forty years ago that illustrates why investment professionals behave as they do. An oil prospector, moving to his heavenly reward, was met by St. Peter with bad news. "You're

> qualified for residence," said St. Peter, "but, as you can see, the compound reserved for oil men is packed. There's no way to squeeze you in." After thinking a moment, the prospector asked if he might say just four words to the present occupants. That seemed harmless to St. Peter, so the prospector cupped his hands and yelled, "Oil discovered in hell." Immediately, the gate to the compound opened and all of the oil men marched out to head for the nether regions. Impressed, St. Peter invited the prospector to move in and make himself comfortable. The prospector paused. "No," he said, "I think I'll go along with the rest of the boys. There might be some truth to that rumor after all."
>
> —WARREN BUFFETT, 1985

John Maynard Keynes defined speculation as "the activity of forecasting the psychology of the market."[5] Keynes went on to say that the speculator must think about what others are thinking about, what others are thinking about the market (and repeat). In what is now called a "Keynesian beauty contest," judges are told not to pick the most beautiful woman but instead to pick the contestant they think the other judges will choose as the most beautiful. The winner of such a contest may be very different than the winner of a traditional beauty contest. Keynes said this about such a contest:

> It's not a case of choosing those [faces] that, to the best of one's judgment, are really the prettiest, nor even those that average opinion genuinely thinks the prettiest. We have reached the third degree where we devote our intelligences to anticipating what average opinion expects the average opinion to be. And there are some, I believe, who practice the fourth, fifth and higher degrees.
>
> —JOHN MAYNARD KEYNES, *GENERAL THEORY,* 1936

How some promoters have learned how to manipulate this process can be illustrated with a story: Once upon a time, a man and his assistant arrived in a very small town and spread the word to the townspeople that the man was willing to buy monkeys for $100 each. The people knew there were many monkeys in the nearby forest and immediately started catching them. Thousands of monkeys were bought at a price of $100 and placed in a large cage. Unfortunately for the townspeople, the supply of monkeys quickly diminished to a point where it took many hours to catch even one.

When the new man announced he would now buy monkeys at a price of $200 per monkey, the town's resident's redoubled their efforts to catch monkeys. But after a few days the monkeys were so hard to find that the townspeople stopped trying to catch any more. The man responded by announcing that he would buy monkeys at $500 after he returned with additional cash from a trip to the big city.

While the man was gone, his assistant told the villagers one by one: "I will secretly sell you my boss' monkeys for $350, and when he returns from the city, you can sell them to him for $500 each."

The villagers bought every single monkey, and they never saw the man or his assistant ever again.

Howard Marks advised that Graham value investors focus on what they know now and not where they are going because, rather obviously, your data about the present is extensive while your data about the future will always be zero. Like Marks in making investment decisions, Munger is focused on what is happening in a given business right now. Projections about the future are scrupulously avoided. Buffett put it this way: "I have no use whatsoever for projections or forecasts. They create an illusion of apparent precision. The more meticulous they are, the more concerned you should be. We never look at projections but we care very much about, and look very deeply, at track records. If a company has a lousy track record but a very bright future, we will miss the opportunity."[6] Munger agreed:

> [Projections] are put together by people who have an interest in a particular outcome, have a subconscious bias, and its apparent

precision makes it fallacious. They remind me of Mark Twain's saying, "A mine is a hole in the ground owned by a liar." Projections in America are often a lie, although not an intentional one, but the worst kind because the forecaster often believes them himself.

—CHARLIE MUNGER, *BUFFETT SPEAKS*, 2007

I don't let others do projections for me, because I don't like throwing up on the desk.

—CHARLIE MUNGER, UNIVERSITY OF CALIFORNIA, SANTA BARBARA, 2003

There is a riddle about people who make short-term forecasts that I have heard many times: Charlie Munger, the Easter Bunny, Superman, and a successful forecaster of an investment bank find themselves in their own corner of a large square-shaped trading floor. In the center of the room is a large stack of $100 bills. If each of them starts racing toward the center of the floor at the same time, who gets the money? The answer is Munger, because the other three don't exist!

By sticking to investing activities that are easy, avoiding questions that are hard, and making decisions based on data that actually exists now, the Graham value investor greatly increases his or her probability of success. Understanding the present is unsurprisingly easier if you know what you are doing and the underlying business is understandable. One must be careful because there are many promoters who can successfully use techniques like "predicting the present" to convey the impression that they can be successful speculators. Predicting the present is, of course, infinitely easier than predicting the future. Consider the following illustrative story about an investor encountering a forecaster. A man piloting a hot-air balloon discovered he had travelled far off course. He took the balloon down to a lower altitude, where he saw that he was above an office building. A man outside the building saw the balloonist and waved.

The balloonist shouted, "Excuse me, can you tell me where I am?"

The man yelled back, "You're in a hot-air balloon, about 150 feet above the headquarters of this investment bank."

The balloonist replied, "You must be a forecaster at the investment bank, then."

Obviously surprised, the man said, "Yes, I am! How did you know that?"

"Well," said the balloonist, "what you told me is technically correct, but it is of no use to anyone."

The best way to determine the value of a business is based on the price a private investor would pay for the entire business. For example, Seth Klarman determines the price *he* would pay for the asset in question and calls that the private market value.

GAMCO Investors defined private market value as follows:

> Private Market Value (PMV) is the value an informed industrialist would pay to purchase assets with similar characteristics. We measure PMV by scrutinizing on- and off-balance-sheet assets and liabilities and free cash flow. As a reference check, we examine valuations and transactions in the public domain. Our investment objective is to achieve an annual return of 10% above inflation for our clients.[7]

While there are many different ways of making this calculation, as will be explained below, all Graham value investors avoid trying to value shares of stock based on popular opinion. An illustration of this point can be found by examining why Munger does not buy gold. Munger does not own gold as an investment because it is impossible to do a bottom-up fundamental valuation, because gold is not an income-producing asset. Gold has speculative value and commercial value, but in Munger's view it has no calculable intrinsic value. Buffett has said that he would be happy to accept a gift of gold, but he would not buy it as an investment. Determining speculative value is all about making predictions about mass psychology, and that is a game

Munger does not want to play. As will be discussed, a private market intrinsic valuation for a Graham value investor requires that the asset generate free cash flow.

Second Principle: Buy at a Significant Discount to Intrinsic Value to Create a Margin of Safety

> The idea of a margin of safety, a Graham precept, will never be obsolete.
>
> —CHARLIE MUNGER, WESCO ANNUAL MEETING, 2003

> No matter how wonderful [a business] is, it's not worth an infinite price. We have to have a price that makes sense and gives a margin of safety considering the normal vicissitudes of life.
>
> —CHARLIE MUNGER, BBC INTERVIEW, 2009

Munger is making the point that if there is a single principle that should rise above all others in the mind of a Graham value investor, it is margin of safety. No one makes this point better than Ben Graham himself:

> Confronted with a challenge to distill the secret of sound investment into three words, we venture the following motto, MARGIN OF SAFETY.
>
> —BEN GRAHAM, *THE INTELLIGENT INVESTOR*, 1949

What is a margin of safety? Ben Graham's definition of a *margin of safety* is "a favorable difference between price on the one hand and indicated or *appraised* [intrinsic] value on the other."[8] Intrinsic value is the present value of future cash flows. Margin of safety reflects the difference between the intrinsic value and the current market price. The purpose of a margin of safety is quite simple according to Graham: "The function of the margin of safety is, in essence, that of rendering unnecessary an accurate estimate of the future."[9] Seth Klarman described the Graham value investing system simply: buy at a bargain defined by a margin of safety and wait. However, as the Tom Petty and the Heartbreakers lyric says, "The waiting is the hardest part."

A margin of safety for investors in public markets is analogous to a safe following distance when driving on the freeway. The intent of both approaches is to avoid having to make predictions. With sufficient distance between you and the car ahead, you must react to what you see in the present moment, but you do not need to predict the actions of the driver ahead of you. If you drive only a few feet behind the speeding car ahead, you need prediction instead of just reaction; otherwise, you are going to crash. Simply put, your objective as a Graham value investor is to buy a share of stock at a sufficiently large bargain that you do not need to predict short-term price movements in the stock market.

The margin of safety principle is natural for a person like Munger, who is trying to succeed by avoiding what is hard (e.g., predicting the future in the short term). He has learned to take the ordinary person's desire to solve hard problems and turn it on its head. Seth Klarman wrote:

> A margin of safety is achieved when securities are purchased at prices sufficiently below underlying value to allow for human error, bad luck, or extreme volatility in a complex, unpredictable and rapidly changing world.
>
> —SETH KLARMAN, *MARGIN OF SAFETY*, 1991

The last point made by Klarman is essential. Making successful predictions about complex systems is a process in which errors are inevitable. Having a margin of safety means that even if you make mistakes, you can still win. And if you do not make mistakes, your win will be even bigger. Munger has a clear view:

> In engineering, people have a big margin of safety. But in the financial world, people don't give a damn about safety. They let it balloon and balloon and balloon.
>
> —CHARLIE MUNGER, BERKSHIRE ANNUAL MEETING, 2003

> If you could take the stock price and multiply it by the number of shares and get something that was one third or less of sellout value, [Ben Graham] would say that you've got a lot of edge going for you. Even with an elderly alcoholic running a stodgy business, this significant excess of real value per share working for you means that all kinds of good things can happen to you. You had a huge margin of safety—as he put it—by having this big excess value going for you.
>
> —CHARLIE MUNGER, UNIVERSITY OF SOUTHERN CALIFORNIA (USC) BUSINESS SCHOOL, 1994

Munger believes that the margin of safety process in investing is similar to processes that exist in engineering. For example, if you are building a bridge, as the engineer you want to make sure that it is significantly stronger than necessary to deal with the very worst case. Buffett wrote once: "When you build a bridge, you insist it can carry 30,000 pounds, but you only drive 10,000 pound trucks across it. And the same idea works in investing."[10] Munger believes investing should be similar. The first rule of investing is: do not make big financial mistakes. The second rule is the same as the first rule.

Behind the margin of safety principle is the simple idea that having a cushion in terms of excess value can protect you against making an error. If you buy at a discount, you have a margin of safety, which will help protect you from making mistakes. This will improve your odds of success. Everyone makes mistakes, so having insurance against those mistakes is wise. Finding an investment opportunity with the right margin of safety is uncommon, so you must be patient. The temptation to do something while you wait is too hard for most people to resist.

As Munger has found over the years, by making certain variables that do not change the four fundamental principles of the Graham value investing system and instead building on top of them, the system has been able to evolve as investing conditions have changed.

> Ben Graham followers . . . started defining a bargain in a different way. And they kept changing the definition so that they could keep doing what they'd always done. And it still worked pretty well.
>
> —CHARLIE MUNGER, USC BUSINESS SCHOOL, 1994

Munger's use of the word *bargain* in the quote immediately above is important. It is not enough for a stock to be beaten down in price or off its highs. What is cheap to buy relative to the past may in fact not be a bargain in the present. To deliver a margin of safety to the Graham value investor, the stock must be worth significantly more than what he or she paid. How significant the bargain must be will be discussed later. The Graham value investor should always remember this admonition: price is what you pay, and value is what you get. It is common for Graham value investors to say things like, "My goal in buying a financial asset is to buy a dollar for 70 cents." When they say this, they do not mean "buy a dollar for seventy cents" precisely, but they do seek a significant discount from intrinsic value. Put simply: when a Graham value investor can buy a dollar for a few dimes less than actual value, he or she can make significant mistakes and still make a profit.

> Ben Graham had a lot to learn as an investor. His ideas of how to value companies were all shaped by how the Great Crash and the Depression almost destroyed him, and he was always a little afraid of what the market can do. It left him with an aftermath of fear for the rest of his life, and all his methods were designed to keep that at bay. I think Ben Graham wasn't nearly as good an investor as Warren Buffett is or even as good as I am. Buying those cheap,

> cigar-butt stocks [companies with limited potential growth selling at a fraction of what they would be worth in a takeover or liquidation] was a snare and a delusion, and it would never work with the kinds of sums of money we have. You can't do it with billions of dollars or even many millions of dollars. But he was a very good writer and a very good teacher and a brilliant man, one of the only intellectuals—probably the only intellectual—in the investing business at the time.
>
> —CHARLIE MUNGER, JASON ZWEIG INTERVIEW, 2014

What Munger is saying above is that what Ben Graham did in applying the concept of a margin of safety in his era was quite different from how investors (like Munger and Buffett) use it today. Look at history. In the aftermath of the Great Depression, Graham was spending most of his time searching for companies "worth more dead than alive."[11] The stock market crash and the Great Depression caused many people to simply give up on owning stocks. For a long time after the Great Depression, some companies could be purchased at less than liquidation value. While these so-called *cigar-butt* companies were common during this period of time, as years passed they became harder to find in major markets. Graham himself said this late in his life, which confuses many people to this day: the fact that public companies were no longer trading at less than liquidation value did not mean that it was no longer possible to use the Graham value investing system successfully.

As a result of the new post-Great Depression environment, Munger and many other Graham value investors began to apply the same Graham value investing principles to businesses that were of high quality instead of businesses trading below liquidation value—and the margin of safety process worked just as well. The variables that supplement the Graham value investing system began to evolve for some investors. Considering the quality of a business when valuing a business will be discussed later in the book.

Walter Schloss, Howard Marks, Seth Klarman, and a few other Graham value investors have stayed closer to Graham's cigar-butt style and instead focused on less-traded markets, given that there are only a small number of cigar-butt opportunities in major public markets. Howard Marks pointed out that "active management has to be seen as the search for mistakes."[12] In his view, it is in less-traded markets and so-called distressed assets where mistakes are most likely to be found.

Third Principle: Make "Mr. Market" Your Servant Rather Than Your Master

> Ben Graham [had] his concept of "Mr. Market." Instead of thinking the market was efficient, he treated it as a manic-depressive who comes by every day. And some days he says, "I'll sell you some of my interest for way less than you think it is worth." And other days, "Mr. Market" comes by and says, "I'll buy your interest at a price that's way higher than you think its worth."
>
> —CHARLIE MUNGER, USC BUSINESS SCHOOL, 1994

In the above statement, Munger is illustrating that Ben Graham's Mr. Market metaphor is as powerful as it is simple. The Graham value investor believes Mr. Market is unpredictably bipolar in the short term; for that reason, when the market is depressed, it will sometimes sell you an asset at a bargain price. Other times, because it is euphoric, the market will pay you more than the asset is worth. Knowing the difference between these two emotional states is of critical importance to the successful use of the Graham value investing system. Mr. Market's emotional problems arise because he is composed of many people who, in the short term, vote to establish a price for an asset based on their emotions and predictions about the predictions and actions of all the other people who make up the market. Ben Graham pointed out that markets are largely composed of such people as "[person] A [who is] trying to decide what B, C, and D are likely to think—with B, C, and D trying to do the same."[13]

For the Graham value investor, it is precisely when Mr. Market is depressed that the greatest opportunities to purchase assets exist. Stocks at that time are likely to be mispriced to an extent that generates a significant bargain. As Ben Graham questioned, why turn something like a drop in stock prices—which is fundamentally advantageous—into something disadvantageous? As long as the fundamentals of the business itself remain in place, a market's short-term views on the price of the shares can be ignored and will be corrected in the long term. This approach reinforces the importance of a fundamental analysis of the business itself. There are essentially three steps in the process: analyze the business to determine intrinsic value, buy the assets at a significant bargain, and wait.

Any discussion about markets inevitably causes arguments related to the so-called *efficient market hypothesis* (EMH). Proponents of the hard version of the EMH believe that investors cannot beat the market because it is always perfectly priced. Unlike EMH proponents, Munger believes that markets are mostly efficient but not always efficient:

> I think it's roughly right that the market is efficient, which makes it very hard to beat merely by being an intelligent investor. But I don't think it's totally efficient at all. And the difference between being totally efficient and somewhat efficient leaves an enormous opportunity for people like us to get these unusual records. It's efficient enough, so it's hard to have a great investment record. But it's by no means impossible. Nor is it something that only a very few people can do. The top 3 or 4 percent of the investment management world will do fine.
>
> —CHARLIE MUNGER, *KIPLINGER*, 2009

One might say that Munger believes in a mostly efficient hypothesis. He believes that the difference between mostly and always efficient is a huge opportunity for a Graham value investor. Stocks are sometimes underpriced and sometimes overpriced. Anyone who invested through the Internet bubble (as I did) and who still thinks that markets are always efficient (a so-called extreme view of market efficiency) is bonkers.

A fundamental premise of the Graham value investing system is that prices will always move up and down in cycles. Graham value investors do not believe these business cycles are predictable in a way that can generate an above-market financial return in the short term. As the business cycle moves prices unpredictably back and forth over time, the reference point is always intrinsic value. Intrinsic value is, in that way, like a mark on a barometer that sets an important reference point. The investor's job is to patiently watch rather than predict price movements and be ready to quickly and aggressively buy at a significant discount to intrinsic value and sometimes sell at an attractive price in relation to intrinsic value. For a Graham value investor, reacting quickly and aggressively to favorable prices when they unpredictably appear is essential. Munger pointed out:

> To Graham, it was a blessing to be in business with a manic-depressive who gave you this series of options all the time.
>
> —CHARLIE MUNGER, USC BUSINESS SCHOOL, 1994

Mr. Market's bipolar nature is his gift to Graham value investors. Occasionally he will present them with great bargains. At other times he'll buy your assets at a premium. Munger's point on this is simple: do not treat Mr. Market as wise; instead, view him as your servant. It is certain that the prices of investment assets will wiggle above and below intrinsic value. Do not try to predict when the wiggle will happen, but rather patiently wait for when it happens. Graham *value* investors price stocks rather than time markets. Patience is a difficult part of the Graham value investing system. If you expect the market to give you enough profit to buy a car or a speedboat next week, you will inevitably fail to achieve your financial goals.

> It's an unfortunate fact that great and foolish excess can come into prices of common stocks in the aggregate. They are valued partly like bonds, based on roughly rational projections of use value in producing future cash. But they are also valued partly like Rembrandt paintings, purchased mostly because their prices have gone up, so far.
>
> —CHARLIE MUNGER, *PHILANTHROPY*, 2009

Falling in with the crowd will put you under the sway of Mr. Market because Mr. Market is the crowd. If you are the crowd, then you cannot, by definition, beat the crowd. Munger believes that short-term price movements are not rationally based, based on always-efficient markets, or predictable with certainty. The best advice is simple; Buffet says, "Be fearful when others are greedy, and be greedy when others are fearful."[14] This is easy to say but hard to do, because it requires courage at the hardest possible time.

> Over many decades, our usual practice is that if [the stock of] something we like goes down, we buy more and more. Sometimes something happens, you realize you're wrong, and you get out. But if you develop correct confidence in your judgment, buy more and take advantage of stock prices.
>
> —CHARLIE MUNGER, WESCO ANNUAL MEETING, 2002

Graham's value investing system is based on the premise that risk (the possibility of losing) is determined by the price at which you buy an asset. The higher the price you pay for an asset, the greater the risk that you will experience a loss of capital. If the price of a stock drops, risk goes down, not up. For this reason, the Graham value investor will often find that price decrease for a given stock is an opportunity to buy more of that stock. Buffett put it this way: "I'm going to buy hamburgers the rest of my life. When hamburgers go down in price, we sing the *Hallelujah* chorus in the Buffett household. When hamburgers go up, we weep."[15]

The paradox facing the ordinary investor is that usually only the biggest investors (huge pension funds, university endowments, and the very wealthy) get access to what Munger refers to as the top 3 to 4 percent investment management. This problem for the ordinary investor is reflected in a variant of an old Groucho Marx joke: you do not want to hire an investment manager that would take you for a client! People managing funds based on Graham value investing principles know that experienced and successful investors are much less likely to panic when a market declines and instead view market declines as an opportunity. Graham value investor Marty Whitman has even said that he does not want people in his fund who do not understand Graham value investing system because he must sell shares when they redeem their ownership interest.

Fourth Principle: Be Rational, Objective, and Dispassionate

> Rationality is not just something you do so that you can make more money; it's a binding principle. Rationality is a really good idea. You must avoid the nonsense that is conventional in one's own time. It requires developing systems of thought that improve your batting average over time.
>
> —CHARLIE MUNGER, WESCO ANNUAL MEETING, 2006

> [An] increase in rationality is not just something you choose or don't choose; it's a moral duty to keep up as much as you reasonably can. It worked so well at Berkshire, not because we were so darned smart to start with—we were massively ignorant. Any of the great successes of Berkshire started with stupidity and failure.
>
> —CHARLIE MUNGER, WESCO ANNUAL MEETING, 2011

The idea of being objective and dispassionate will never be obsolete.
—CHARLIE MUNGER, BERKSHIRE ANNUAL MEETING, 2003

As the above quotes indicate, over the years Munger has repeatedly said that the most important quality that makes anyone a successful investor is the ability to make rational thoughts and decisions. It is difficult to overestimate how important being rational is to the Graham value investing system. Rationality is the best antidote to making psychological and emotional errors. During an interview, Munger once recalled that a person sitting next to him at a dinner party asked him, "Tell me, what one quality accounts for your enormous success?" Munger replied, "I'm rational. That's the answer. I'm rational." This rationality is something he works hard to cultivate, as will be explained shortly. Being rational is neither simple nor easy.

While Graham value investors do not try to predict the behavior of other people, they do spend a lot of time trying to keep their own behavior from getting in the way of being rational, objective, and dispassionate. The best Graham value investors understand that if you think things through from the simplest building blocks in a step-by-step process and employ techniques like checklists, which reinforce the Graham value investing system, you can avoid making most mistakes—or at least making new mistakes. Most of this book will be devoted to this fourth principle of the Graham value investing system.

3
WORLDLY WISDOM

What is elementary, worldly wisdom? Well, the first rule is that you can't really know anything if you just remember isolated facts and try and bang 'em back. If the facts don't hang together on a latticework of theory, you don't have them in a usable form.

—CHARLIE MUNGER, UNIVERSITY OF SOUTHERN CALIFORNIA (USC) BUSINESS SCHOOL, 1994

You must know the big ideas in the big disciplines, and use them routinely—all of them, not just a few. Most people are trained in one model—economics, for example—and try to solve all problems in one way. You know the old saying: to the man with a hammer, the world looks like a nail. This is a dumb way of handling problems.

—CHARLIE MUNGER, WESCO ANNUAL MEETING, 2000

All the wisdom of the world is not to be found in one little academic department. That's why poetry professors, by and large, are so unwise in a worldly sense. They don't have enough models in their heads.

—CHARLIE MUNGER, USC BUSINESS SCHOOL, 1994

> What are the models? Well, the first rule is that you've got to have multiple models—because if you just have one or two that you're using, the nature of human psychology is such that you'll torture reality so that it fits your models.
>
> —CHARLIE MUNGER, USC BUSINESS SCHOOL, 1994

Munger has adopted an approach to business and life that he refers to as *worldly wisdom*. Munger believes that by using a range of different models from many different disciplines—psychology, history, mathematics, physics, philosophy, biology, and so on—a person can use the combined output of the synthesis to produce something that has more value than the sum of its parts. Robert Hagstrom wrote a wonderful book on worldly wisdom entitled *Investing: The Last Liberal Art*, in which he states that "each discipline entwines with, and in the process strengthens, every other. From each discipline the thoughtful person draws significant mental models, the key ideas that combine to produce a cohesive understanding. Those who cultivate this broad view are well on their way to achieving worldly wisdom."[1]

It is clear that Munger loves to learn. He actually has fun when he is learning, and that makes the worldly wisdom investing process enjoyable for him. This is important because many people do not find investing enjoyable, especially when compared to gambling, which science has shown can generate pleasure via chemicals (e.g., dopamine) even though it is an activity with a negative net present value. What Munger has done is created a system—worldly wisdom—that allows him to generate the same chemical rewards in an activity that has a positive net present value. When you learn something new, your brain gives itself a chemical reward, which motivates you to do the work necessary to be a successful investor. If you do this work and adopt a worldly wisdom mindset, Munger believes you will create an investing edge over other investors.

In developing his worldly wisdom approach, Munger uses what he calls a "lattice of mental models." What is a mental model? Herbert Simon captured the idea:

> A large part of the difference between the experienced decision maker and the novice in these situations is not any particular intangible like "judgment" or "intuition." If one could open the lid, so to speak, and see what was in the head of the experienced decision maker, one would find that he had at his disposal repertoires of possible actions; that he had checklists of things to think about before he acted; and that he had mechanisms in his mind to evoke these, and bring these to his conscious attention when the situations for decisions arose.
>
> —HERBERT SIMON, *MCKINSEY QUARTERLY*, 1986

The lattice metaphor was also carefully chosen by Munger to convey the idea that the multiple models needed to acquire worldly wisdom must be interconnected.

> You've got to have models in your head. And you've got to array your experience—both vicarious and direct—on this latticework of models.
>
> —CHARLIE MUNGER, USC BUSINESS SCHOOL, 1994

Understanding the worldly wisdom methodology is made easier if you see it applied in an example. To illustrate the method, Munger gave the example of a business that raises the price of its product and yet sells more of that product. This would appear to violate the rule of supply and demand as taught in economics. However, if one thinks about the discipline of psychology, one might conclude that the product is a *Geffen good*, which people desire more of at higher prices. Or one could conclude that low prices signal poor quality to buyers and that raising prices will result in more sales. Alternatively, you can look for bias caused by incentives and discover that what has actually happened in his example is that the seller has bribed the purchasing agents of the purchasers.

Munger described a situation in which this actually happens:

> Suppose you're the manager of a mutual fund, and you want to sell more. People commonly come to the following answer: You raise

> the commissions which, of course, reduces the number of units of real investments delivered to the ultimate buyer, so you're increasing the price per unit of real investment that you're selling the ultimate customer. And you're using that extra commission to bribe the customer's purchasing agent. You're bribing the broker to betray his client and put the client's money into the high-commission product.
>
> —CHARLIE MUNGER, UCS BUSINESS SCHOOL, 2003

No one can know everything, but you can work to understand the big, important models in each discipline at a basic level so they can collectively add value in a decision-making process. Simply put, Munger believes that people who think very broadly and understand many different models from many different disciplines make better decisions and are therefore better investors. This view should not be a surprise because he believes that the world is composed of many complex systems that are constantly interacting:

> You've got a complex system and it spews out a lot of wonderful numbers that enable you to measure some factors. But there are other factors that are terribly important, [yet] there's no precise numbering you can put to these factors. You know they're important, but you don't have the numbers. Well, practically (1) everybody overweighs the stuff that can be numbered, because it yields to the statistical techniques they're taught in academia, and (2) doesn't mix in the hard-to-measure stuff that may be more important. That is a mistake I've tried all my life to avoid, and I have no regrets for having done that.
>
> —CHARLIE MUNGER, UCS BUSINESS SCHOOL, 2003

In Munger's view, it is better to be *worldly wise* than to spend lots of time working with a single model that is precisely wrong.

A multiple-model approach that is only approximately right will produce a far better outcome in anything that involves people or a social system. While making the case for a lattice of mental models approach (described here shortly), Robert Hagstrom pointed out that Munger is providing support for those who advocate for a wide-ranging liberal arts education. Munger argued persuasively that activities like reading great books can help someone become a better investor:

> The theory of modern education is that you need a general education before you specialize. And I think to some extent, before you're going to be a great stock picker, you need some general education.
>
> —CHARLIE MUNGER, USC BUSINESS SCHOOL, 1994

In the language of Wharton Professor Philip Tetlock, Munger is a "fox" (who knows a little about a lot) rather than a "hedgehog" (who knows a lot about very little).[2] Among the foxes one may encounter in life, Munger is truly special. He knows a lot about a lot, and he knows a little about nearly everything. Bill Gates made this point when he said, "Charlie Munger is truly the broadest thinker I have ever encountered."[3] Buffett added that Munger has "the best 30-second mind in the world. He goes from A to Z in one move. He sees the essence of everything before you even finish the sentence."[4]

Munger believes that thinking broadly in many disciplines makes you a better thinker because everything is literally related.

> You have to realize the truth of biologist Julian Huxley's idea that "Life is just one damn relatedness after another." So you must have the models, and you must see the relatedness and the effects from the relatedness.
>
> —CHARLIE MUNGER, *POOR CHARLIE'S ALMANACK*, 2005

Understanding disciplines like biology, psychology, chemistry, physics, history, philosophy, or engineering will make you a better investor. Munger believes:

> People calculate too much and think too little.
>
> —CHARLIE MUNGER, BERKSHIRE ANNUAL MEETING, 2002

Munger's breadth of knowledge is something that is naturally part of his character but also something that he intentionally cultivates. In his view, to know nothing about an important subject is to invite problems. Both Munger and Buffett set aside plenty of time each day to just think. Anyone reading the news is provided with constant reminders of the consequences of not thinking. Thinking is a surprisingly underrated activity. Researchers published a study in 2014 that revealed that approximately a quarter of women and two-thirds of men chose electric shocks over spending time alone with their own thoughts.[5] Munger would likely say that people who cannot be alone with their own thoughts are terrible candidates to become successful investors.

Munger's speeches and essays are filled with the thoughts of great people from the past and present from many different domains. Munger is also careful to set aside a lot of time in his schedule for reading. To say he loves books is an understatement. Buffett has said that Munger has read hundreds of biographies, as just one example. He is very purposeful in his approach to worldly wisdom, preferring not to fill his calendar with appointments and meetings. "You could hardly find a partnership in which two people settle on reading more hours of the day than in ours." Buffett added, "Look, my job is essentially just corralling more and more and more facts and information, and occasionally seeing whether that leads to some action."[6]

Munger illustrates the idea of worldly wisdom by pointing out that many professionals often think only about their own discipline, believing that whatever it is that they do for a living will cure all problems. A nutritionist may feel as if he or she can cure anything, for example. A chiropractor may believe he or she can cure cancer. Learning from others is essential, according to Munger.

> I believe in the discipline of mastering the best that other people have ever figured out. I don't believe in just sitting down and trying to dream it all up yourself. Nobody's that smart.
>
> —CHARLIE MUNGER, STANFORD LAW SCHOOL, 1998

It is critical for a person who desires to be wise to think broadly and learn from others. Munger has said many times that someone who is really smart but has devoted all of their time to being an expert in a narrow area may be dangerous to themselves and others. Examples of this include macroeconomists who study the economy but are disastrous when investing their own portfolios and marketing experts who may think that most all business problems can be solved through marketing. Financiers tend to think similarly about their own profession. Too many people believe that what they do at work is hard and what others do is easy.

Munger believes that the best approach to dealing with problems can be found in adopting a multidisciplinary approach:

> You may say, "My God, this is already getting way too tough." But, fortunately, it isn't that tough—because eighty or ninety important models will carry about 90 percent of the freight in making you a worldly wise person. And, of those, only a mere handful really carry very heavy freight.
>
> —CHARLIE MUNGER, USC BUSINESS SCHOOL, 1994

This reference to "eighty or ninety important models" has caused people to ask Munger for a complete list of these important models. While Munger identified many models in the discipline of psychology in his famous "The Psychology of Human Misjudgment" speech and mentioned other models on an ad-hoc basis, he has never prepared a complete list covering all disciplines.

Munger believes that by learning to recognize certain dysfunctional decision-making processes, an investor can learn to make fewer mistakes. He also believes that no matter how hard someone works and learns, mistakes cannot be completely eliminated. The best one can hope for is to reduce their frequency and, hopefully, their magnitude. Munger elaborated:

> Man's imperfect, limited-capacity brain easily drifts into working with what's easily available to it. And the brain can't use what it

> can't remember or when it's blocked from recognizing because it's heavily influenced by one or more psychological tendencies bearing strongly on it . . . the deep structure of the human mind requires that the way to full scope competency of virtually any kind is to learn it all to fluency—like it or not.
>
> —CHARLIE MUNGER, HARVARD UNIVERSITY, 1995

> I constantly see people rise in life who are not the smartest, sometimes not even the most diligent, but they are learning machines. They go to bed every night a little wiser than they were when they got up, and boy, does that help, particularly when you have a long run ahead of you. . . . So if civilization can progress only with an advanced method of invention, you can progress only when you learn the method of learning. Nothing has served me better in my long life than continuous learning. I went through life constantly practicing (because if you don't practice it, you lose it) the multidisciplinary approach and I can't tell you what that's done for me. It's made life more fun, it's made me more constructive, it's made me more helpful to others, and it's made me enormously rich. You name it, that attitude really helps.
>
> —CHARLIE MUNGER, USC LAW SCHOOL, 2007

In looking at a decision, Munger believes that it is wise to ask questions. Have dysfunctional decision-making heuristics from psychology caused an error? Are there approaches one can use to find those mistakes? Munger likes to use a model from algebra and invert problems to find a solution. Looking for models that can reveal and explain mistakes so one can accumulate worldly wisdom is actually lots of fun. It is like a puzzle to be solved.

A lattice approach is, in effect, a double-check on the investing process. But instead of just two checks, you are checking the result over and over. Munger believes that by going over your decision-making process and carefully using skills, ideas, and models from many disciplines, you can more consistently *not be stupid*. You will always make some bone-headed mistakes even if you're careful, but his process is designed to decrease the probability of those mistakes.

To make sure he is taking advantage of as many models as possible, Munger likes checklists:

> You need a different checklist and different mental models for different companies. I can never make it easy by saying, "Here are three things." You have to derive it yourself to ingrain it in your head for the rest of your life.
>
> —CHARLIE MUNGER, BERKSHIRE ANNUAL MEETING, 2002

As part of his worldly wisdom approach to life, Munger focuses on learning from mistakes:

> You can learn to make fewer mistakes than other people—and how to fix your mistakes faster when you do make them.
>
> —CHARLIE MUNGER, HARVARD UNIVERSITY, 1995

> Terribly smart people make totally bonkers mistakes.
>
> —CHARLIE MUNGER, USC BUSINESS SCHOOL, 1994

> I don't want you to think we have any way of learning or behaving so you won't make mistakes.
>
> —CHARLIE MUNGER, USC BUSINESS SCHOOL, 1994

Munger learned about business in the best way possible: by participating in it on a firsthand basis, and by sometimes making mistakes and sometimes being successful. Through the process of making mistakes and succeeding or failing in the real world (i.e., getting feedback from the market), you can learn and establish sound business judgment. Many Berkshire investments have been valuable in that they have taught Buffett and Munger what not to do. For Buffett, buying a New England textile mill in the 1960s was in some ways a mistake. It was a lousy business that was not worth putting any new capital into, because it would never generate more return on capital investment than alternative investments available to Buffett. When Berkshire paid too much for Conoco Phillips or bought US Airways, it was a mistake. Buying Dexter Shoes was also a multi-billion dollar mistake for Berkshire. In doing their due-diligence analysis for Dexter shoes, Buffett and Munger made the mistakes of not making sure the business had a *moat* and being too focused on what they thought was an attractive purchase price. Buffett said once about Dexter Shoes: "What I had assessed as durable competitive advantage vanished within a few years."[7] Capitalism inherently means that others will always be trying to replicate any business that is profitable. You are always in a battle to keep what you have. Dexter Shoes lost that battle quickly. If you make a mistake, capitalism's "competitive destruction" forces will expose it swiftly and, sometimes, brutally.

> I don't think it's necessary to be as dumb as we were.
>
> —CHARLIE MUNGER, BERKSHIRE ANNUAL MEETING, 2011

> I like people admitting they were complete stupid horses' asses. I know I'll perform better if I rub my nose in my mistakes. This is a wonderful trick to learn.
>
> —CHARLIE MUNGER, BERKSHIRE ANNUAL MEETING, 2011

Munger has said repeatedly that he made more mistakes earlier in life than he is making now. One of his early mistakes was to own a company that made electrical transformers. He has also said that he has found himself in real estate ventures that would only be enjoyed by a masochist. He seems to have more tolerance for mistakes in real estate than other areas of business. The idea of building things as opposed to just trading stocks has a particular appeal to Munger.

Munger believes that one great way to avoid mistakes is to own a business that is simple to understand, given your education and experience. He pointed out: "Where you have complexity, by nature you can have fraud and mistakes."[8] This approach echoes the view of Buffett, who likes challenges that are the business equivalent of netting fish in a barrel.

Buffett has said that if you cannot explain why you failed after you have made a mistake, the business was too complex for you. In other words, Munger and Buffett like to understand why they made a mistake so they can learn from the experience. If you cannot understand the business, then you cannot determine what you did wrong. If you cannot determine what you did wrong, then you cannot learn. If you cannot learn, you will not know what you're doing, which is the real cause of risk.

> Forgetting your mistakes is a terrible error if you're trying to improve your cognition. Reality doesn't remind you. Why not celebrate stupidities in both categories?
>
> —CHARLIE MUNGER, WESCO ANNUAL MEETING, 2006

Munger admits that he still makes mistakes even after many decades as a business person and investor. Among the worst mistakes Munger has made are things that he didn't do.

> The most extreme mistakes in Berkshire's history have been mistakes of omission. We saw it, but didn't act on it. They're huge mistakes—we've lost billions. And we keep doing it. We're getting better at it. We never get over it. There are two types of mistakes: 1) doing nothing—what Warren calls "sucking my thumb" and 2) buying with an eyedropper things we should be buying a lot of.
>
> —CHARLIE MUNGER, BERKSHIRE ANNUAL MEETING, 2001

> Our biggest mistakes were things we didn't do, companies we didn't buy.
>
> —CHARLIE MUNGER, *FORTUNE* MAGAZINE, 1998

Munger and Buffett's decision to not invest in Wal-Mart is just one example of a mistake of omission. Buffett has said that just this one mistake with Wal-Mart cost them $10 billion. Similarly, in 1973, Tom Murphy offered to sell a group of television stations to Berkshire for $35 million and Berkshire Hathaway declined. "That [failure to buy those television stations] was a huge mistake of omission,"[9] Buffett has admitted.

Munger has chosen the word *wisdom* purposefully because he believes that mere knowledge, especially from only one domain, is not enough. To be wise, one must also have experience, common sense, and good judgment. How one actually applies these things in life is what makes a person wise.

4
THE PSYCHOLOGY OF HUMAN MISJUDGMENT

HUMANS HAVE DEVELOPED simple rules of thumb called *heuristics*, which enable them to efficiently make decisions. Heuristics are essential; without them it would be impossible to make the decisions required to get through a normal day. They allow people to cope with information and computation overload and to deal with risk, uncertainty, and ignorance. Unfortunately, these heuristics can sometimes result in tendencies to do certain things that are dysfunctional. Of course, having a tendency is not destiny. That people will tend to do something does not mean that they will always do so, that they cannot learn to overcome the tendency, or that all people have the same tendency. Everyone, including Munger, must be careful not to fall prey to certain (often dysfunctional) tendencies.

Particularly in the context of human activities that were not a part of most of our evolutionary past as a species (such as investing), heuristics can produce one boneheaded mistake after another. Professor Richard Zeckhauser, whom Munger admires greatly for his decision-making processes when playing bridge and as an investor, wrote:

"individuals tend to extrapolate heuristics from situations where they make sense to those where they do not."[1]

> Bias [arises] from the nonmathematical nature of the human brain in its natural state as it deals with probabilities employing crude heuristics, and is often misled.
>
> —CHARLIE MUNGER, HARVARD UNIVERSITY, 1995

Why does this happen? James Montier pointed out:

> The simple truth is that we aren't adapted to face the world as it is today. We evolved in a very different environment, and it's that ancestral evolutionary environment that governs the way in which we think and feel. We can learn to push our minds into alternative ways of thinking, but it isn't easy, as we have to overcome the limits to learning posed by self-deception. In addition, we need to practice the reframing of data into more evolutionary, familiar forms if we are to process it correctly.
>
> —JAMES MONTIER, *DARWIN'S MIND*, 2006

Heuristics conserve scarce mental and physical resources, but the same process, which is sometimes beneficial, can lead people to harmful systematic errors.

> Tendencies are probably much more good than bad. Otherwise, they wouldn't be there, working pretty well for man, given his condition and his limited brain capacity. So the tendencies can't be simply washed out automatically and shouldn't be. . . . Tendency is not always destiny, and knowing the tendencies and their antidotes can often help prevent trouble that would otherwise occur.
>
> —CHARLIE MUNGER, HARVARD UNIVERSITY, 1995

One way to understand Munger better is to relate his thinking to a personal story. My case involved something that happened a few years ago. For a few months, I had been having slight pain in my bicep muscles near my elbows. My doctor said the injury probably resulted from lifting weights. One night in January of 2013, I was sleeping soundly when I was jolted awake by much more significant pain in both of my arms. I immediately thought, "I am having a small heart attack. I need to get to an emergency room." I woke my wife and asked her to get dressed quickly and get in the car. As we were driving to the hospital, the painful sensations in my arms started to go away. It was at that point that I started convincing myself that pain in my arms was not really from a heart attack. I am sure I was subconsciously thinking, "I have a busy schedule next week. I can't have a heart attack right now. This pain is most likely nothing. I probably just hurt myself in the gym. Who has a heart attack without any chest pain?" At that point I said to my wife, "Maybe we should go home. Are you going to insist that we go to the hospital?" My wife did insist and we went to the emergency room. I might have argued with her, but at that moment I reminded myself about Munger and Buffett's approach to risk:

> Take the probability of loss times the amount of possible loss from the probability of gain times the amount of possible gain. That is what we're trying to do. It's imperfect, but that's what it's all about.
>
> —WARREN BUFFETT, BERKSHIRE ANNUAL MEETING, 1989

Going to the emergency room for tests on my heart function was clearly wise because the amount of possible loss was so massive even if the probability was small (which it was not, given the symptoms). After thinking about this formula, I knew I needed to get to the hospital. In this case, rationality (and my wife) overcame psychological denial, optimism, and other negative decision-making tendencies. It turned out that my pain was from a small heart attack, and three days later, I was in the operating room for a triple-bypass operation on my heart.

The reality is that we all tell ourselves false stories to avoid the truth. Even if you spend a lot of time studying behavioral economics, you can only improve your skills on the margin. You will always make mistakes. Nobel Prize winner Daniel Kahneman, who has spent most of his professional life researching behavioral economics, has said: "Except for some effects that I attribute mostly to age, my intuitive thinking is just as prone to overconfidence, extreme predictions, and the planning fallacy."[2] Even though you cannot be perfect, you can get marginally better at avoiding mistakes and have an edge in the market over people who do not understand Munger's tendencies and other aspects of behavioral economics.

Investing is less than a zero-sum game due to fees, costs, and expenses relative to the market. If you are buying an investment, by definition someone else is selling. Either the buyer or the seller is making a mistake, unless the price of the asset does not change and the result is a draw. In other words, one truism about investing is this: for you to find a significant mistake, someone else must be making a mistake too.

> Investors operate within what is for the most part a zero-sum game. While it's true that the value of all companies usually increases over time with economic growth, market outperformance by one investor is necessarily offset by another's underperformance.
>
> —SETH KLARMAN, BAUPOST GROUP LETTER, 2005

For example, if you understand dysfunctions that are caused by behavioral economics phenomena and the other person does not, then you have a potential edge. The best Graham value investors spend a lot of time thinking about possible sources of dysfunctional decision-making and emotional errors. Other people's errors create opportunities for the Graham value investor. As Professor Bruce Greenwald of Columbia Business School has noted, "There's a lot of behavioral finance confirming Ben Graham's original judgment."[3]

Taking a close look at Munger's explanation of some major psychological tendencies is well worth your time. Munger is aware that his list of heuristics is far from complete. Readers of this book are advised to read other books and articles that expand on this list and deal with heuristics like mental accounting, sunk cost, ambiguity, regret, and framing, just to name a few.

1. Reward and Punishment Superresponse Tendency

> Almost everyone thinks he fully recognizes how important incentives and disincentives are in changing cognition and behavior. But this is not often so. For instance, I think I've been in the top 5 percent of my age cohort almost all my adult life in understanding the power of incentives, and yet I've always underestimated that power. Never a year passes but I get some surprise that pushes a little further my appreciation of incentive superpower.
>
> —CHARLIE MUNGER, HARVARD UNIVERSITY, 1995

> Upton Sinclair said it best of all. He said, "It's very hard to get a man to believe non-X when his way of making a living requires him to believe X." On a subconscious level, your brain plays tricks on you and you think [that] what is good for the true little me is what you should believe.
>
> —CHARLIE MUNGER, HARVARD-WESTLAKE SCHOOL, 2010

> The iron rule of nature is that you get what you reward for. If you want ants to come, put sugar on the floor.
>
> —CHARLIE MUNGER, WESCO ANNUAL MEETING, 2001

Reward and punishment superresponse tendency relates to what psychologists call *reinforcement* and what economists call *incentives*. A classic example of this tendency causing problems in investing may happen when a financial advisor is able to earn a big sales commission for selling clients offerings, such as certain types of annuities. The financial incentives available to the advisor can turn an otherwise kindly, churchgoing, community-minded person into a perversely motivated shark. This misalignment of incentives is why it is wise to retain a fee-based financial planner and to make sure that he or she is not receiving hidden rebates and sales commissions. Munger gave another example:

> Everyone wants to be an investment manager, raise the maximum amount of money, trade like mad with one another, and then just scrape the fees off the top. I know one guy; he's extremely smart and a very capable investor. I asked him, "What returns do you tell your institutional clients you will earn for them?" He said, "20 percent." I couldn't believe it, because he knows that's impossible. But he said, "Charlie, if I gave them a lower number, they wouldn't give me any money to invest!" The investment-management business is insane.
>
> —CHARLIE MUNGER, JASON ZWEIG INTERVIEW, 2014

Munger's story reminds me of another story:

A man of the church died and was waiting in line at the pearly gates. Ahead of him was a money manager. Saint Peter asked the money manager, "Who are you? What did you do that might cause me to admit you to heaven?"

"I'm Joe Smith. I managed the money of thousands of people," the man replied.

Saint Peter consulted his list and said to the money manager, "Take this silk robe and gold staff and enter heaven."

Now it was the minister's turn. "I am Father Joseph Flannigan, most recently of Saint Patrick's in New York City."

Saint Peter consulted his list and said, "Take this cotton robe and wood staff and enter heaven."

"Just a minute," said Father Flannigan. "That man was a money manager—he received a silk robe and gold staff, but I only get a cotton robe and wood staff? How can this be?"

"Up here, we make assignments based on results," said Saint Peter. "While you preached, people slept. His clients prayed."

What benefits an investor most in avoiding problems such as those Munger discusses above is a financial planner who "eats his own cooking" with incentives, which causes him to suffer and benefit right alongside his client.

> An example of a really responsible system is the system the Romans used when they built an arch. The guy who created the arch stood under it as the scaffolding was removed. It's like packing your own parachute.
>
> —CHARLIE MUNGER, BERKSHIRE ANNUAL MEETING, 1993

It is easy to find examples of how improper incentives are damaging civilization by reading the day's news. An example of this problem and a potential solution was raised by Nassim Taleb:

> Instead of relying on thousands of meandering pages of regulation, we should enforce a basic principle of "skin in the game" when it comes to financial oversight. "The captain goes down with the ship; every captain and every ship." In other words, nobody should be in a position to have the upside without sharing the downside, particularly when others may be harmed.
>
> —NASSIM TALEB, 2012

Munger sees this problem today reflected in the fact that accountants have been turned into policemen by law and regulation due to the fact that managers are not keeping themselves far away from activities that might be unethical or illegal. Holding managers legally responsible for their actions would be a great place to start.

Munger believes that structuring compensation incentives is critical. If the right structure exists, then a seamless web of deserved trust can be created which lessens problems related to this tendency. For example, it is surprising how many people fail to recognize how performance suffers if you pay someone in advance rather than after the work has been completed. It's precisely because of the dangers of misaligned incentives that Munger and Buffett chose to make compensation decisions themselves, whereas they delegate almost all management responsibilities.

2. Liking/Loving Tendency

> Admiration also causes or intensifies liking or love. With this "feedback mode" in place, the consequences are often extreme, sometimes even causing deliberate self-destruction to help what is loved.
>
> —CHARLIE MUNGER, HARVARD UNIVERSITY, 1995

Munger believes that people tend to ignore or deny the faults of people they love and also tend to distort facts to facilitate that love. He believes we are more influenced by people we like, and perhaps more importantly by people who genuinely like us. There are obviously positive aspects to this tendency for society, but they rarely have a place in making investment decisions. You may like or even love your friend or relative, but that does not mean that you should trust him or her with your money. Loaning money to relatives is fraught with danger. It is usually a far better idea to simply give away money to needy friends and relatives—or, if you do make a loan, to never expect it back. Relatives and friends in receipt of your money as a loan too often acquire a short-term and fuzzy/selective memory. Another example of this tendency arises when people fall in love with a company and make investing mistakes about that company as a result of that love. Even if you love your employer, it is very risky to have too much of your savings in the stock of a single company. One way that some companies leverage this tendency is to have their salespeople sell to people they know at parties. Tupperware parties are a classic example of this principle in action.

One valuable check on this liking/loving tendency is to seek out wise people who are not afraid to disagree with you. Munger likes to say that a year in which you do not change your mind on some big idea that is important to you is a wasted year.

3. Disliking/Hating Tendency

> Avoid evil, particularly if they're attractive members of the opposite sex.
>
> —CHARLIE MUNGER, BERKSHIRE ANNUAL MEETING, 2004

The disliking/hating tendency is the inverse of the previous tendency. Munger believes that life is too short to do business with people you don't like. He also refuses to invest in certain companies that sell goods and services that he does not like for ethical reasons. As an example, Munger and Buffett avoid investing in casinos.

Munger believes that the disliking/hating tendency can sometimes be dysfunctional even if you ignore the ethical aspects. For example, the fact that a job candidate attended a rival college of your alma mater should not influence your hiring decision. Taking a factor like that into account is simply not rational. In other words, Munger believes it is sensible to pass judgment on a company or person for ethical reasons, but one must be careful not to pass judgment on a company or person based on irrational associations. Family members do not fall outside of the disliking/hating tendency. Munger quoted Buffett on this point: "A major difference between rich and poor people is that the rich people can spend more of their time suing their relatives."[4]

Compliance professionals, including some politicians and religious leaders, have learned to manipulate people into making decisions using this tendency. If someone attempts to manipulate your behavior, you should stay rational and separate how you feel about one thing from how you feel about something else that is related. If someone seems to like or admire you, it may be a ruse to secure your compliance with something they desire. The skill needed to sort out whether a person is genuine is acquired with experience—the cause of good judgment is usually experiences involving bad judgment. Some people seem to never learn and some people seem to be born with good judgment, and this is one of life's great mysteries.

4. Doubt-Avoidance Tendency

> [It's] counterproductive for a prey animal that is threatened by a predator to take a long time in deciding what to do.
>
> —CHARLIE MUNGER, *POOR CHARLIE'S ALMANACK*, 2005

Researchers believe that the doubt-avoidance tendency exists because a brain's processing load can be substantially reduced if a person rejects doubt. Daniel Kahneman considers doubt-avoidance tendency to be a System 1 activity, which Michael Mauboussin described as follows: "System 1 is your experiential system. It's fast. It's quick. It's automatic and really difficult to control. System 2 is your analytical system: slow, purposeful, deliberate, but malleable."[5] When it comes to investments, avoiding doubt can get a person into serious trouble. One example is the people who thought, "Why investigate an asset manager like Bernard Madoff when avoiding doubt is so much easier? After all, he managed money for many important people. Surely they looked carefully into his operations and background."

The confidence of entrepreneurs bolstered by doubt-avoidance tendency creates positive benefits for society in the aggregate by generating productivity and genuine growth in the economy, even if legions of entrepreneurs may fail. Nassim Taleb put it this way: "Most of you will fail, disrespected, impoverished, but we are grateful for the risks you're taking and the sacrifices you're making for the sake of the economic growth of the planet and pulling others out of poverty. You're the source of our antifragility. Our nation thanks you."[6]

5. Inconsistency-Avoidance Tendency

> The brain of man conserves programming spaces by being reluctant to change.
>
> —CHARLIE MUNGER, HARVARD UNIVERSITY, 1995

People are reluctant to change even when they have been given new information that conflicts with what they already believe. Inconsistency-avoidance tendency is another often-useful heuristic because starting each day with a fresh mind about everything requires too much processing power. Unfortunately, as is the case with every heuristic, what is mostly helpful can sometimes be harmful. The adverse effects of this tendency can be made worse when it appears in combination with the previously discussed doubt-avoiding tendency. The desire to resist any change in a given conclusion or belief is particularly strong if a person has invested a lot of effort in reaching that conclusion or belief and/or if the change will result in something that is unpleasant. This is a major reason why progress in many professions tends to advance "one funeral at a time." An example of this phenomenon can be found in the many companies which refused to recognize that personal computers or mobile phones were a threat to their business.

Absence of the inconsistency-avoidance tendency among some people operates to benefit society. For example, company founders who are not wedded to old ideas can sometimes create innovative new businesses more easily. As another example, an executive may cling to an idea he or she has publicly advocated, even after facts come to light proving the idea false. One way to avoid this problem is to be very careful about what you say in public. Also, be aware that once you say something in public, you may be blind to disconfirming evidence. Mark Twain's statement comes to mind on this tendency: "All you need in this life is ignorance and confidence; then success is sure."[7] Some entrepreneurs often don't know enough to think that something can't be done, so once in a while they actually do something that is completely unexpected. As the old saying goes, even a blind squirrel finds a nut once in a while.

6. Curiosity Tendency

Curiosity can provide both fun and wisdom, and occasionally trouble.
—CHARLIE MUNGER, *POOR CHARLIE'S ALMANACK*, 2005

> I was born innately curious. If that doesn't work for you, figure out your own damn system.
>
> —CHARLIE MUNGER, WESCO ANNUAL MEETING, 2010

> Experience tends to confirm a long-held notion that being prepared, on a few occasions in a lifetime, to act promptly in scale, in doing some simple and logical thing, will often dramatically improve the financial results of that lifetime. A few major opportunities, clearly recognizable as such, will usually come to one who continuously searches and waits, with a curious mind that loves diagnosis involving multiple variables. And then all that is required is a willingness to bet heavily when the odds are extremely favorable, using resources available as a result of prudence and patience in the past.
>
> —CHARLIE MUNGER, WESCO ANNUAL MEETING, 1996

Many things in life involve tradeoffs. A source of what is good in life can also be a source of what is bad in life. That inevitable tradeoff applies to curiosity—and there is nothing like failure and mistakes to teach a person the right approach to curiosity. The wise investor will acquire a sort of muscle memory about curiosity based on actual experience. Curiosity about life and restraint about difficult decisions are part of Munger's approach to life. Seeking more information about a topic, even though it has no present value to a person, is a natural human drive. One can speculate that having this information has option value. However, the price of too much curiosity can be high. Finding the right balance in things involving tradeoffs like curiosity is a key part of acquiring wisdom.

An example of a problem arising from too much curiosity would be a tycoon who is curious to see whether he or she can finally be the person to make a long-term profit in the airline business. There's an old joke on this plan: "How do you become a millionaire? Start as a billionaire and buy an airline." Buffett himself jokes that he has a toll-free number he can call which will talk him out of investing in airlines whenever he gets the urge. Curiosity can also cause an investor to engage in too many activities or a business owner to offer too many products and services, but end up failing by offering none. Startup founders can end up repeatedly "pivoting" their business (i.e., changing business models or business categories) into oblivion if they overload on curiosity. At the same time, curiosity can lead to important breakthroughs for a business. Striking the right balance on something like curiosity requires judgment.

7. Kantian Fairness Tendency

> Modern acculturated man displays and expects from others a lot of fairness.
>
> —CHARLIE MUNGER, HARVARD UNIVERSITY, 2005

> The craving for perfect fairness causes a lot of terrible problems in system function. Some systems should be made deliberately unfair to individuals because they'll be fairer on average for all of us.
>
> —CHARLIE MUNGER, UNIVERSITY OF CALIFORNIA, SANTA BARBARA (UCSB), 2003

> Tolerating a little unfairness to some to get a greater fairness for all is a model I recommend to all of you.
>
> —CHARLIE MUNGER, UCSB, 2003

Humans will often act irrationally to punish people who are not fair. In other words, investors may react irrationally when presented with a situation that they feel is unfair. For example, some people would rather lose money in an investment than see another person benefit from unfairness. Another way this tendency may arise is when people sometimes reject systems that are not fair to an individual, even though the system in question is best for a group or society. Munger points to such a rule in the U.S. Navy which dictates that your career is over if you make a big mistake (e.g., if your ship goes aground) even if it was not your fault. Munger believes that the rule is good for society because it creates incentives for the naval officer to make sure that this does not happen, even though it may not be fair to the individual. However, this is hard for many people to accept due to the fairness heuristic, even though it may be logically correct.

8. Envy/Jealousy Tendency

> A member of a species designed through evolutionary process to want often scarce food is going to be driven strongly toward getting food when it first sees food. And this is going to occur often and tend to create some conflict when the food is seen in the possession of another member of the same species. This is probably the evolutionary origin of the envy/jealousy tendency that lies so deep in human nature.
>
> —CHARLIE MUNGER, UNIVERSITY OF SOUTHERN CALIFORNIA (USC), 1994

> The idea of caring that someone is making money faster [than you] is one of the deadly sins. Envy is a really stupid sin because it's the only one you could never possibly have any fun at. There's a lot of pain and no fun. Why would you want to get on that trolley?
>
> —CHARLIE MUNGER, WESCO ANNUAL MEETING, 2003

> Missing out on some opportunity never bothers us. What's wrong with someone getting a little richer than you? It's crazy to worry about this.
>
> —CHARLIE MUNGER, WESCO ANNUAL MEETING, 2005

> Here's one truth that perhaps your typical investment counselor would disagree with: if you're comfortably rich and someone else is getting richer faster than you by, for example, investing in risky

> stocks, so what?! Someone will always be getting richer faster than you. This is not a tragedy.
>
> —CHARLIE MUNGER, WESCO ANNUAL MEETING, 2000

> Well, envy/jealousy made, what, two out of the Ten Commandments? Those of you who have raised siblings . . . or tried to run a law firm or investment bank or even a faculty, you know about envy. I've heard Warren say a half a dozen times, "It's not greed that drives the world, but envy."
>
> —CHARLIE MUNGER, HARVARD UNIVERSITY, 1995

> Remember, [Moses] said you couldn't even covet your neighbor's donkey.
>
> —CHARLIE MUNGER, CNBC INTERVIEW, 2014

The dangers of envy are a frequent Munger topic, as you can see from the extensive list of quotations above. Munger believes that envy is such a powerful emotion because for most of human history people have lived in an environment in which severe scarcity was the normal situation. He believes that very primal emotions are triggered when humans see someone with something they don't have, often causing dysfunctional thoughts and actions. Envy is an emotion designed to motivate people to acquire attributes and possessions that increase evolutionary fitness. Now that there is less scarcity in the world, envy has lost much of its value. Instead of motivating people for emotional fitness, envy just makes people unhappy. Munger's point on envy is simple: nothing good comes from envy. He believes that envy is a completely wasted emotion that a person should work hard to avoid.

Major problems arising from envy happen because people increase risk when they envy the financial success of someone else. The stock market is not going to deliver you a sports car next week simply because your neighbor just acquired one and you're envious. Promoters of all sorts will point to the possessions of others in an attempt to motive you to comply with their requests. Just saying no to envy is the best approach.

9. Reciprocation Tendency

> The automatic tendency of humans to reciprocate favors and disfavors has long been noticed as extreme.
>
> —CHARLIE MUNGER, HARVARD UNIVERSITY, 1995

Professor Robert Cialdini has pointed out that, "People will help if they owe you for something you did in the past to advance *their* goals. That's the rule of reciprocity."[8] The reverse is also true if you have done something that negatively affects a person. The urge to reciprocate favors and disfavors is so strong that even someone smiling at you is hard not to reciprocate. The indebted feeling that humans have when they receive a gift tends to make a person feel uncomfortable until he or she can extinguish the debt. The urge to reciprocate in some way so as to cancel the debt is so strong that it can even make people give up substantially more than they would if the process was fully rational. In other words, the desire to reciprocate often results in an unequal exchange of value. Compliance professionals have learned to use this feeling of reciprocity to their advantage. For example, a Hare Krishna fundraiser has been trained to give away a "gift," like a flower, when he or she approaches a person for a donation. The free weekend at a time-share condominium has a similar purpose for the salespeople who offer it to potential buyers. The investment promoter who gives away a "free" lunch wants the person who attends the event to reciprocate in a very disproportionate way. As an aside, a person who enjoys the free lunch and does not take the bait and buy the investment may be disparaged by the promoter as a "plate licker."

10. Influence-from-Mere-Association Tendency

> Think how association, pure association, works. Take Coca-Cola Company (we're the biggest shareholder). They want to be associated with every wonderful image: heroics in the Olympics,

> wonderful music, you name it. They don't want to be associated with presidents' funerals and so forth.
>
> —CHARLIE MUNGER, HARVARD UNIVERSITY, 1995

Humans are programmed to be pattern seekers. They look for patterns to obtain what they believe is guidance about how to make decisions. For example, when a well-known actor pitches an investment firm's services on television, it is likely that the actor knows next to nothing about investing; yet people tend to respond positively merely because the actor may be associated with something positive, like acting skill. Unfortunately, people can be misled by mere association too easily, and that can lead to investing errors. This tendency is similar to the liking tendency, except only association is required. Liking tendency is more about being blind to the faults of people we like. With association theory, the compliance professional is trying to get you to do something like buy a financial service because it is endorsed or used by a famous actor. Because compliance professionals know this human weakness, advertisers spend huge amounts of money to associate their products and services with favorable images. Munger believes that advertisers want customers to respond to images in a manner similar to Pavlov's dog. For example, See's Candies wants you to associate their products with pleasant memories from the past. Also, the fact that an engagement ring from Acme is not perceived to have the same value as an engagement ring from Tiffany is not an accident. However, a celebrity endorsement of an investment should have no impact on your investing decisions.

Influence from association can also work in reverse, such as when a person is unfairly connected to something unfavorable they did not cause. An example of this is the Persian messenger syndrome (also known as "shoot the messenger"). There is significant danger inherent in this syndrome because people, often executives or politicians, may surround themselves with people who only tell them what they want to hear. Munger pointed to Bill Paley of CBS as an example of someone who put himself in a cocoon of unreality and suffered a major business failure as a result.

11. Simple, Pain-Avoiding Psychological Denial

One should recognize reality even when one doesn't like it.
—CHARLIE MUNGER, BERKSHIRE ANNUAL MEETING, 2000

A friend of our family had a super-athlete, super-student son who flew off a carrier in the north Atlantic and never came back, and his mother, who was a very sane woman, just never believed that he was dead. And, of course, if you turn on the television, you'll find the mothers of the most obvious criminals that man could ever diagnose, and they all think their sons are innocent. That's simple psychological denial. The reality is too painful to bear, so you just distort it until it's bearable. We all do that to some extent, and it's a common psychological misjudgment that causes terrible problems.
—CHARLIE MUNGER, HARVARD UNIVERSITY, 1995

A projection prepared by anybody who stands to earn a commission or an executive trying to justify a particular course of action will frequently be a lie—although it's not a deliberate lie in most cases. The man has come to believe it himself. And that's the worst kind. Projections should be handled with care, particularly when they're being provided by someone who has an interest in misleading you.
—CHARLIE MUNGER, BERKSHIRE ANNUAL MEETING, 1995

Failure to handle psychological denial is a common way for people to go broke.
—CHARLIE MUNGER, HARVARD UNIVERSITY, 1995

People hate to hear bad news or anything inconsistent with their existing opinions and conclusions. For this reason, if something is potentially painful, the human brain often goes to work trying to deny reality. Nobel Prize-winning psychologist Daniel Kahneman believes that "[people do not invest even] the smallest amount trying to actually figure out what they've done wrong—not an accident: they don't want to know."[9] For example, smart investors should have known that it was not possible for Bernard Madoff's fund to generate not only positive but amazingly consistent returns. What were Madoff's investors thinking when, month after month, they received financial statements that were positive with little volatility? Madoff investors were so happy with the results that they simply distorted reality. In short, the investors liked the results they saw on the statements from Madoff so much that they went into a state of psychological denial. Even a professor who wrote a scholarly book on gullibility was an investor in the Bernard Madoff Ponzi scheme.

A common example of psychological denial happens when people make projections about a potential investment. Weirdly, sometimes the fewer facts there are to support a well-told story, the more believable it may be for certain investors. Only when real facts start to appear do these people start to question the story. Daniel Kahneman pointed this out: "It's all too easy to tell stories that make sense of one's life in retrospect."[10] This is why it's particularly dangerous to short a so-called *story stock*. Another example that Munger has cited for the psychological denial tendency at work is academics who love the beauty of mathematics. The mathematics of certainty (e.g., trigonometry, geometry) is so much better put together than the messy world of statistics and decision making under conditions of uncertainty. The love of this beautiful math can cause these academics to ignore the fact that the assumptions which form the basis of their mathematics are flawed.

12. Excessive Self-regard Tendency

> We don't like complexity and we distrust other systems and think it many times leads to false confidence. The harder you work, the more confidence you get. But you may be working hard on something that is false.
>
> —CHARLIE MUNGER, *SEEKING WISDOM*, 2003

People tend to vastly overestimate their own capabilities. This is a huge problem for many investors and a major part of the reason why staying within a circle of competence is so important. This book has made the point repeatedly that the most effective way to genuinely reduce risk is to know what you're doing. Part of being a genuine expert is to know the limits of your own competence. Unfortunately, this is far too often not the case. Daniel Kahneman believes: "Confidence is a feeling, one determined mostly by the coherence of the story and by the ease with which it comes to mind, even when the evidence for the story is sparse and unreliable. The bias toward coherence favors overconfidence. An individual who expresses high confidence probably has a good story, which may or may not be true."[11]

In responding to a survey, 70 percent of students said they were above average in leadership ability, and only 2 percent rated themselves as below average in relation to their peers.[12] In rating their athletic skills, 60 percent saw themselves above the median and only 6 percent below the median. Companies are not immune from this excessive self-regard tendency, including Berkshire's portfolio companies:

> [GEICO] got to thinking that, because they were making a lot of money, they knew everything. And they suffered huge losses. All they had to do was to cut out all the folly and go back to the perfectly wonderful business that was lying there.
>
> —CHARLIE MUNGER, USC BUSINESS SCHOOL, 1994

In making his point about the excessive self-regard tendency, Munger noted that way more than half of Swedish drivers think they are above-average drivers:

> Investment counselors make Swedish drivers sound like depressives. Virtually every investment expert's public assessment is that he is above average, no matter what is the evidence to the contrary.
>
> —CHARLIE MUNGER, SPEECH TO FOUNDATION OFFICERS, 1998

Investors themselves share this same overconfidence. In 2012, a major fund group released a survey indicating that 91 percent of their active investors believe that they would beat or at least equal the returns of the market over the next year.[13] This, of course, is mathematically impossible.

13. Over-Optimism Tendency

> In the 4th century B.C., Demosthenes noted that "what a man wishes, he will believe." And in self-appraisals of prospects and talents it's the norm, as Demosthenes predicted, for people to be ridiculously over-optimistic.
>
> —CHARLIE MUNGER, *PHILANTHROPY*, 1999

Investor over-optimism—and its evil twin, over-pessimism—are what make Mr. Market bipolar. The good news for people who can keep their level of optimism at rational levels is that the unpredictable but inevitable gyrations between these two states create opportunities for Graham value investors. Staying rationally optimistic as the market gyrates is very difficult. Only a small number of people can do it successfully. Even experts who spend their lives studying behavioral economics can fall prey to the over-optimism and over-pessimism tendencies. For example, Nobel Prize winner Daniel Kahneman wrote this:

> One of our biases is that we can ignore the lessons of experience. A group of people compiling a report will estimate they can do it in a year, even though every other similar report has taken comparable groups five years. . . . When I started the book I told Richard Thaler (the author of Nudge) that I had 18 months to finish it. He laughed hysterically and said, "You have written about that, haven't you? It's not going to work the way you expect." "How long did it take you?" I ask. "Four years, and it was very painful."[14]

If someone who has spent his life studying dysfunctional decision-making falls prey to the same problems he studies (e.g., overoptimism), these tendencies are indeed strong.

14. Deprival Super-Reaction Tendency

> The deprival super-reaction syndrome of man helps cause much ruin as people's cognition is distorted as a result of their suffering losses and near misses.
>
> —CHARLIE MUNGER, STANFORD LAW SCHOOL, 1998

> Your brain doesn't naturally know how to think the way Zeckhauser knows how to play bridge. For example, people do not react symmetrically to loss and gain. Well, maybe a great bridge player like Zeckhauser does, but that's a trained response.
>
> —CHARLIE MUNGER, HARVARD UNIVERSITY, 1995

> I mean people are really crazy about minor decrements down. . . . Huge insanities can come from just subconsciously overweighing the importance of what you're losing or almost getting and not getting.
>
> —CHARLIE MUNGER, HARVARD UNIVERSITY, 1995

The deprival super-reaction tendency is more commonly called *loss aversion*, and it can cause investors to irrationally avoid risk when they face potential for gain, but irrationally seek risk when there is a potential for loss. In other words, people tend to be too conservative in seeking gains and too aggressive in seeking to avoid losses. The most important point to remember about this tendency is that it causes investors to do things like sell stocks too early and hold on to them for too long. It is very common for investors to hold on to losing stocks in the hope that somehow the price will rise and they will somehow break even. As another example of this tendency at work, many investors were so traumatized by stock losses after the

2007 financial crisis that they completely missed the subsequent rally in the markets.

> One of prospect theory's most important contributions to finance is loss aversion, the idea that, for most people, losses loom larger than corresponding gains. The empirical evidence suggests we feel losses about two to two-and-a-half times more than we feel gains.
>
> —MICHAEL MAUBOUSSIN, *AVER AND AVERSION*, 2005

A good example of how loss aversion creates dysfunctional behavior happens at the racetrack. People betting on horses bet more and more on longshots as the day goes on. This happens because the majority of people have lost money because, with the odds stacked in favor of the house, the racetrack has the betting edge. Because people are averse to losses, as the day progresses they bet more on long shots in the hope that they can recoup their losses and perhaps generate a gain before they go home.

15. Social-Proof Tendency

> Big-shot businessmen get into these waves of social proof. Do you remember some years ago when an oil company bought a fertilizer company, and every other major oil company practically ran out and bought a fertilizer company? And there was no more damned reason for all these oil companies to buy fertilizer companies, but they didn't know exactly what to do, and if Exxon was doing it, it was good enough for Mobil, and vice versa. I think they're all gone now, but it was a total disaster.
>
> —CHARLIE MUNGER, HARVARD UNIVERSITY, 1995

This brings to mind Ben Graham's paradoxical observation that good ideas cause more investment mischief than bad ideas. He

> had it right. It's so easy for us all to push a really good idea to wretched excess, as in the case of the Florida land bubble or the "nifty fifty" corporate stocks. Then mix in a little "social-proof" (from other experts), and brains (including ours) often turn to mush.
>
> —CHARLIE MUNGER, HARVARD UNIVERSITY, 1995

Humans have a natural tendency to follow a herd of other humans. In other words, because humans do not have unlimited time and complete information, they tend to copy the behavior of other humans. Cialdini put it this way: "One means we use to determine what is correct is to find out what other people think is correct. We view a behavior as more correct . . . to the degree we see others performing it."[15]

Social-proof tendency is one major cause of financial bubbles. Social-proof tendency is often used by fraudsters. For example, Bernie Madoff was a master at using social-proof tendency to get investors to give him their money. He worked hard to make it known that he managed money for famous people who were considered to be "smart money." One odd fact of life is that people tend to follow famous investors into deals even though the famous person is not even remotely famous for his or her investing skill. Learning to ignore the crowd and think independently is a trained response.

Munger is a big proponent of independent thinking in investing. In thinking independently, it's wise to remember Seth Klarman's view that a Graham value investor is a marriage between a contrarian and a calculator. Falling in with the crowd due to social proof means it is mathematically impossible to outperform the market. Independent thinking can be an opportunity to arbitrage the tendency of people to follow the crowd. Profit can be made by sometimes zigging when the crowd zags if you see a wager in which the odds are substantially in your favor. It is not enough to be contrarian; you must also be sufficiently right in terms of the magnitude of the positive outcome that you outperform the markets.

16. Contrast-Misreaction Tendency

> Because the nervous system of man does not naturally measure in absolute scientific units, it must instead rely on something simpler. The eyes have a solution that limits their programming needs: the contrast in what is seen is registered. And as in sight, so does it go, largely, in the other senses. Moreover, as perception goes, so goes cognition. The result is man's Contrast-Misreaction Tendency. Few psychological tendencies do more damage to correct thinking. Small-scale damages involve instances such as man's buying an overpriced $1,000 leather dashboard merely because the price is so low compared to his concurrent purchase of a $65,000 car. Large-scale damages often ruin lives, as when a wonderful woman having terrible parents marries a man who would be judged satisfactory only in comparison to her parents. Or as when a man takes wife number two, who would be appraised as alright only in comparison to wife number one.
>
> —CHARLIE MUNGER, HARVARD UNIVERSITY, 1995

Munger points to real estate brokers who may first show clients unattractive properties at inflated prices in order to increase the probability that clients will buy a subsequently viewed property at an inflated price as an example of this tendency. In other words, if your real estate broker starts the tour with a dog of a deal, they are very likely trying to train you to buy what is coming next. No one should buy an investment merely because it's better than the lousy one you just saw or owned. Similarly, when you buy an asset, it should be the best investment of all the investments that are available to you anywhere. For example, the fact that Y is a better stock than X is not enough information to make an investing decision. Is Y the best investment of all the investments you could possibly make anywhere? Thinking about the world through an opportunity-cost lens is a simple but often-ignored idea.

17. Stress-Influence Tendency

Here my favorite example is the great Pavlov. He had all these dogs in cages, which had all been conditioned into changed behaviors, and the great Leningrad flood came and it just went right up and the dog is in a cage. And the dog had as much stress as you can imagine a dog ever having. And the water receded in time to save some of the dogs, and Pavlov noted that they'd had a total reversal of their conditioned personality.

—CHARLIE MUNGER, HARVARD UNIVERSITY, 1995

Some level of stress can actually increase a person's performance. However, people under too much stress tend to make really lousy decisions. For example, a salesperson with highly developed compliance skills can cause people to make big investment mistakes by putting the sales prospect under stress. One of the more infamous examples of this sales approach is the sale of a time-share in a resort condominium. Often, a friendly salesperson operates in tandem with a person who specializes in applying stress (this is known as a "good-cop/bad-cop" approach). I would rather drop a cinder block on my foot than accept a free weekend in a time-share condominium. Do not make decisions while under stress. It's just that simple.

18. Availability-Misweighing Tendency

The great algorithm to remember in dealing with this tendency is simple: an idea or a fact is not worth more merely because it's easily available to you.

—CHARLIE MUNGER, HARVARD UNIVERSITY, 1995

Investors have a tendency to make decisions based on what they can easily recall. The more vivid and memorable the event, fact, or phenomenon may be, the more likely it will be used by the investor in making a decision—even if what is being recalled is not the best data on which to make a decision. For example, if stocks have recently dramatically fallen in a market crash, investors tend to be afraid to buy, even though it may be the very best time to buy. The year 2002 was an excellent time to buy stocks, but the memory of the crash of the stock market after the collapse of the Internet bubble was so vivid that only people who, like Munger, had trained themselves to overcome this tendency were able to use that opportunity to reap big investing rewards.

Similarly, if someone has recently and publicly cashed in with a huge financial return on a startup, other people who learn about that success tend to overestimate their chances of success in creating their own startup. People are also more likely to buy stocks if the markets have been rising in price significantly. This psychological tendency to misweigh what is easily recalled is a major reason why people are attracted to lotteries despite the dismal odds of winning, as they have seen other ordinary people win a lottery on the news. Lotteries promote this love by distributing pictures to the press of people holding oversized checks.

19. Use-It-or-Lose-It Tendency

> All skills attenuate with disuse. I was a whiz at calculus until age twenty, after which the skill was soon obliterated by total nonuse.
>
> —CHARLIE MUNGER, HARVARD UNIVERSITY, 1995

This tendency is pretty simple to understand; a skill degrades unless it is practiced regularly. For example, flying an airplane is not something you should do once in a while. If you're not flying often as a pilot, you should not be flying as a pilot. Similarly, investing is not something you want to do once in a while. In the context of investing, it is both a fact of life and a shame that so many people spend more time picking out an appliance than picking an investment or investment fund. To be a successful investor, a person must regularly devote the necessary time and effort. Even if you once felt that you knew a lot about investing, it does not mean your skills are current. Maintaining a circle of competence requires constant work and diligence. As a 2014 study concluded,

> We find that interventions to improve financial literacy explain only 0.1% of the variance in financial behaviors studied, with weaker effects in low-income samples. Like other education, financial education decays over time; even large interventions with many hours of instruction have negligible effects on behavior 20 months or more from the time of intervention.
>
> —DANIEL FERNANDES, JOHN LYNCH, AND RICHARD NETEMEYER, 2014

20. Drug-Misinfluence Tendency

> We all know talented people who have ruined their lives abusing either alcohol or drugs—and often both.
>
> —CHARLIE MUNGER, HARVARD-WESTLAKE SCHOOL, 1986

> Three things ruin people: drugs, liquor, and leverage.
>
> —CHARLIE MUNGER, WESCO ANNUAL MEETING, 2009

> The four closest friends of my youth were highly intelligent, ethical, humorous types, favored in person and background. Two are long dead, with alcohol a contributing factor, and a third is a living alcoholic—if you call that living. While susceptibility varies, addiction can happen to any of us, through a subtle process where the bonds of degradation are too light to be felt until they are too strong

> to be broken. And I have yet to meet anyone, in over six decades of life, whose life was worsened by overfear and overavoidance of such a deceptive pathway to destruction.
>
> —CHARLIE MUNGER, HARVARD-WESTLAKE SCHOOL, 1986

Everyone makes mistakes, but Munger has repeatedly said that staying away from the really big mistakes, like cocaine and heroin, is vital. As an analogy, Munger has pointed out that if you are floating down a river and there are really dangerous whirlpools that are killing many people on a daily basis, you do not go anywhere near that whirlpool. Munger also pointed to alcoholism as a major cause of failure in life. His point on substance abuse is simple: why play dice with something that can ruin your life forever? His timeless advice in every setting is to avoid situations with a massive downside and a small upside (negative optionality). This is the reciprocal of his investing advice: seek bets with a huge upside and a small downside (positive optionality). Other tendencies, such as psychological denial, can prevent people from getting the help they need, making matters worse for people with drug or alcohol problems. A drug or alcohol problem can quickly become a self-reinforcing negative feedback loop, which is impossible to escape.

21. Senescence-Misinfluence Tendency

> Some people remain pretty good in maintaining intensely practiced old skills until late in life, as one can notice in many a bridge tournament. . . . Continuous thinking and learning, done with joy, can somewhat help delay what is inevitable.
>
> —CHARLIE MUNGER, HARVARD UNIVERSITY, 1995

Munger's own life is support for the view that if you have the right genetics and consciously work hard to remain physically and mentally active, you can stay sharp as you age. Luck certainly plays an important part in outcomes related to aging, but there is no excuse for not working to do the best you can with the luck you have. Staying active is essential to mental and physical health. As just one example, nothing is more fun for people like Munger than learning—and nothing helps learning more than reading. When it comes to health, do not be passive. As an example of Munger not accepting deteriorating health passively, when he was confronted with a diagnosis that he might lose all of his sight, he began studying Braille. It is far better to wear out from work than rust out from inactivity.

22. Authority-Misinfluence Tendency

> You get a pilot and a co-pilot. The pilot is the authority figure. They don't do this in airplanes, but they've done it in simulators. They have the pilot do something where the co-pilot, who's been trained in simulators a long time—he knows he's not to allow the plane to crash—they have the pilot do something where an idiot co-pilot would know the plane was going to crash, but the pilot's doing it, and the co-pilot is sitting there, and the pilot is the authority figure. 25 percent of the time, the plane crashes. I mean, this is a very powerful psychological tendency.
>
> —CHARLIE MUNGER, HARVARD UNIVERSITY, 1995

People tend to follow people who they believe are authorities, especially when they face risk, uncertainty, or ignorance. Professor Cialdini described the authority tendency this way: "When people are uncertain . . . they don't look inside themselves for answers—all they see is ambiguity and their own lack of confidence. Instead, they look outside for sources of information that can reduce their uncertainty. The first thing they look to is authority."[16] Compliance professionals have learned to convey their authority before they start working to influence people. For example, they will talk about their professional degrees, awards, and achievements. They might even talk about how wealthy they are or refer to other authorities who endorse their expertise. Professor Cialdini noted that titles, expensive clothing, and the trappings of a professional all tend to be effective in conveying authority. Michael Mauboussin pointed out that, "The individual who comes across as more authoritative is actually more believable. People are much more comfortable deferring to the person in the pinstripe suit with the PowerPoint slides."[17] In the famous Milgram experiments, people complied with instructions to apply electric shocks to other people in an experiment because the person giving the command was wearing a laboratory coat and looked like an authority.[18] Unfortunately, someone like a stock promoter in a fancy suit and expensive car may seem like an authority to some investors. The church official who asserts that the investment is ethical may overcome rather obvious ethical concerns merely because he or she seems to be an authority on ethics.

23. Twaddle Tendency

> It's obvious that if a company generates high returns on capital and reinvests at high returns, it will do well. But this wouldn't sell books, so there's a lot of twaddle and fuzzy concepts that have been introduced that don't add much.
>
> —CHARLIE MUNGER, WESCO ANNUAL MEETING, 2000

> I think the notion that liquidity of tradable common stock is a great contributor to capitalism is mostly twaddle. The liquidity gives us these crazy booms, so it has as many problems as virtues.
>
> —CHARLIE MUNGER, BERKSHIRE ANNUAL MEETING, 2004

The definition of *twaddle* is simple; it is speech or writing that is silly or not true; nonsense. *Prattle* has an equally simple definition: to talk in a foolish way. What Munger is saying is that people tend to spend a lot of time on meaningless activities. To illustrate the point, he gives the example of a honeybee that knows that the flowers are directly over the hive but has no way to convey that using its dance-based signaling. Despite the fact that no information is being conveyed, the honeybee will still dance in a way that conveys nothing.

> I try to get rid of people who always confidently answer questions about which they don't have any real knowledge. To me they are like the bee dancing its incoherent dance. They are just screwing up the hive.
>
> —CHARLIE MUNGER, WESCO MEETING NOTES, 1998

Like the honeybee with flowers located directly overhead, many experts who are faced with a situation they know nothing about will prattle and twaddle anyway. In Munger's view, people too often confuse twaddle and prattle with importance and value. Even worse, many people pay fees to consultants and advisors for twaddle and prattle. Of course, the hardest thing to spot is when you are telling yourself twaddle, because the easiest person to fool is always yourself.

24. Reason-Respecting Tendency

> Reason-Respecting Tendency is so strong that even a person's giving of meaningless or incorrect reasons will increase compliance with his orders and requests. This has been demonstrated in psychology experiments wherein "compliance practitioners" successfully jump to the head of the lines in front of copying machines by explaining their reason: "I have to make some copies." This sort of unfortunate byproduct of Reason-Respecting Tendency is a conditioned reflex, based on a widespread appreciation of the importance of reasons. And, naturally, the practice of laying out various claptrap reasons is much used by commercial and cult "compliance practitioners" to help them get what they don't deserve.
>
> —CHARLIE MUNGER, HARVARD UNIVERSITY, 1995

Compliance professionals know they will have more success in convincing people to act against their personal interest if the person is given a reason for the action, even if the reason is absurd. As an example, so-called boiler-room operators pitching sham investments have their cold-calling salespeople working from scripts heavy with reasons designed to get people to comply with requests to buy into scams, like promoted penny stocks. Salespeople have learned they can raise their closing percentage if they give a fake reason that the buyer may lose the opportunity to buy if they wait any longer. A scam artist might say, "You should buy this penny gold-mining stock because it is wedding season in India" or "The weather in South Africa has been poor, and that is great news for gold mines in the United States." Yet another example would be a meaningless pattern in a chart of stock prices that has been given a name, like a "death cross." Even panhandlers know to put the reason they need money on their cardboard signs. Just because someone gives you a reason for doing something stupid does not make it smart. A story might help readers understand this point:

> A Wall Street analyst and his client, a stock speculator, went to the horse races together one day. The speculator suggested that they bet $5,000 on a horse. The analyst explained that he would instead research each horse and only bet after doing a careful analysis. "You are too theoretical," said the speculator walking off to place his bet.

As it happened, the horse did finish first. The speculator triumphantly exclaimed, "I told you. I have a secret formula!"

"What's your secret formula?" the analyst asked.

"It's simple. I have two kids, two and six years old. I sum up their ages and I bet on number nine."

"But, two plus six is eight," protested the analyst.

"I told you, you are too theoretical!" the broker replied.

25. Lollapalooza Tendency

> An investment decision in the common stock of a company frequently involves a whole lot of factors interacting. . . . The one thing that causes the most trouble is when you combine a bunch of these together, you get this lollapalooza effect.
>
> —CHARLIE MUNGER, HARVARD UNIVERSITY, 1995

The lollapalooza tendency is the tendency to get extreme confluences of psychological tendencies acting in favor of a particular outcome. Munger believes that all of the tendencies, forces, and phenomena described previously in this book can interact with each other in self-reinforcing ways, which make the output of the whole of what is interacting greater than the sum of the parts. Munger calls this process a lollapalooza. Because a lollapalooza involves feedback, its impact can be nonlinear in nature and is inherently unpredictable. Munger has pointed out that that the impact of a lollapalooza involves vastly more than simple addition of the components that are interacting. Munger instead described it as similar to a "nuclear explosion." One reason why prediction with certainty with respect to a lollapalooza is impossible is that a certain critical mass is required. In other words, the process that creates a lollapalooza will either reach critical mass, as in a nuclear reaction, or will never reveal itself.

Munger has identified a number of lollapalooza examples. In his view, the 2007 financial crisis "was a lollapalooza event—a confluence of causes; that is how complex systems work."[19] Long-Term Capital Credit Management's financial implosion was also a lollapalooza event, according to Munger. He also thinks the rise and fall of the Internet bubble was a lollapalooza. Another example of a lollapalooza is a Tupperware party where social proof, liking, and other tendencies are used by the company to get people to buy products. Munger wrote an essay about the brand power of Coca-Cola, describing its tremendous value as being the outcome of a lollapalooza phenomenon. An open-outcry auction is another example of a lollapalooza:

> Well, the open-outcry auction is just made to turn the brain into mush: you've got social proof, the other guy is bidding, you get reciprocation tendency, you get deprival super-reaction syndrome, and the thing is going away. . . . I mean, it just absolutely is designed to manipulate people into idiotic behavior.
>
> —CHARLIE MUNGER, HARVARD UNIVERSITY, 1995

The techniques that an auctioneer can use for benevolent purposes in a charity auction can also be used by a criminal to convince people to invest in scams. Buffett's advice for these open outcry auctions is simple: "Don't go."

A lollapalooza is not inherently good or bad. Sometimes a lollapalooza effect can be used for benevolent purposes.

> The system of Alcoholics Anonymous: a 50 percent no-drinking rate outcome when everything else fails? It's a very clever system that uses four or five psychological systems at once toward, I might say, a very good end.
>
> —CHARLIE MUNGER, HARVARD UNIVERSITY, 1995

However, Munger also believes that the same forces used by Alcoholics Anonymous to help people with alcoholism have been used by cults for evil. For example, Charles Manson and other cult leaders learned to manipulate people through a lollapalooza process. Clearly, Bernie Madoff used multiple self-reinforcing tendencies, like social proof and envy, to motivate the victims of his Ponzi scheme. Munger believes Moonie "conversions" are achieved by combining psychological tendencies. On the positive side, Munger also cites Buffett's investing record as an example of a positive lollapalooza.

> A confluence of factors in the same direction caused Warren's success. It's very unlikely that a lollapalooza effect can come from anything else.
>
> —CHARLIE MUNGER, WESCO ANNUAL MEETING, 2007

I hope that reading this book will help you generate your own positive lollapalooza.

5
THE RIGHT STUFF

IN HIS BIOGRAPHY of Warren Buffett, Roger Lowenstein pointed out that Buffett's "genius was largely a genius of character—of patience, discipline and rationality. . . . His talent sprang from his unrivaled independence of mind and ability to focus on his work and shut out the world." The same things can be said about Charlie Munger. Both of these investors are extraordinary individuals. There is only one Charlie Munger and one Warren Buffett. Having said that, you don't need to have exactly the same attributes as these two longtime partners to marginally improve your skills as an investor. You can improve your ability to read, think, learn, avoid mistakes, and pay attention to the personal attributes that drive success.

This chapter identifies a few of the attributes that make up "the right stuff" of a successful investor, as identified over the years by Munger. Although he almost certainly feels that other attributes are important too, the ones in this chapter have been discussed most extensively and frequently by Munger. He admits that he struggles with these attributes, just like everyone else. No one is perfect, including Munger. Therefore, my intent is not to create a subtext of "just do it," since doing these things in our daily lives is genuinely hard.

1. Patient

Success means being very patient but aggressive when it's time.

—CHARLIE MUNGER, BERKSHIRE ANNUAL MEETING, 2004

It would be nice if [finding great investments] happened all the time. Unfortunately, it doesn't.

—CHARLIE MUNGER, BERKSHIRE ANNUAL MEETING, 2005

We don't feel some compulsion to swing. We're perfectly willing to wait for something decent to come along. In certain periods, we have a hell of a time finding places to invest our money.

—CHARLIE MUNGER, BERKSHIRE ANNUAL MEETING, 2001

Patience combined with opportunity is a great thing to have. My grandfather taught me that opportunity is infrequent and one has to be ready when it strikes. That's what Berkshire is.

—CHARLIE MUNGER, WESCO ANNUAL MEETING, 2011

We are both very action prone when it's obvious.

—CHARLIE MUNGER, CNBC INTERVIEW, 2014

The probability that you will encounter an asset that can be purchased at a significant discount from private market value is significantly higher when Mr. Market is fearful. However, Munger believes that predicting exactly when this will happen is impossible. Instead, his approach is to wait for bargains to appear, focusing on whatever is happening in the present moment. Therefore, a Graham value investor must be patient. This can be very difficult, as there is a tendency to think that the level of activity is somehow correlated with value.

"Don't just sit there; do something," is precisely the wrong advice for a Graham value investor.

Buffett has said that the stock market is designed to transfer money "from the active to the patient."[1] If you are patient, rational, and otherwise follow the Graham value investing system, Mr. Market will inevitably deliver his financial gifts to you. You cannot predict when it will happen, but you can certainly wait patiently for the gift to be transferred to you. In this sense, the Graham value investing system is a discovery-based process rather than a prediction-based process.

Munger told a story about a young person who once asked him how to get rich. He described the conversation as follows:

> We get these questions a lot from the enterprising young. It's a very intelligent question: you look at some old guy who is rich and you ask, "How can I become like you, except faster?"
>
> —CHARLIE MUNGER, WESCO ANNUAL MEETING, 2003

The approach Munger suggested was to patiently "slug it out" day-by-day, preparing for occasional fast spurts. The idea that one can make a lot of money in just a few instances after being patient in other instances is something Munger developed playing poker in the U.S. Army. Munger ascribes no small amount of his financial success in investing to the time he spent playing poker and bridge.

> The right way to think is the way Zeckhauser plays bridge. It's just that simple.
>
> —CHARLIE MUNGER, HARVARD LAW SCHOOL, 1995

At a fundamental level, investing is just one form of making a bet. It is essential, however, that the bet be made in a way that is investing (net present value positive) rather than gambling (net present value negative). As I noted previously, investing is a probabilistic exercise and experience with other games of chance can be helpful. The great bridge player and Harvard professor Richard Zeckhauser pointed out:

> Bridge requires a continual effort to assess probabilities in at best marginally knowable situations, and players need to make hundreds of decisions in a single session, often balancing expected gains and losses. But players must also continually make peace with good decisions that lead to bad outcomes, both one's own decisions and those of a partner. Just this peacemaking skill is required if one is to invest wisely in an unknowable world.
>
> —RICHARD ZECKHAUSER, 2006

Buffett believes that bridge shares many characteristics with investing. Every hand is different, yet what has happened in the past is meaningful. In investing, you must make inferences about every bid or card, as well as cards that are not played. Also, as in bridge, you can benefit from having a great partner and strong interpersonal skills. Understanding probability and statistics is essential in both card playing and investing. Munger put it simply:

> If you don't get elementary probability into your repertoire, you go through a long life like a one-legged man in an ass-kicking contest.
>
> —CHARLIE MUNGER, UNIVERSITY OF SOUTHERN CALIFORNIA (USC) SCHOOL OF BUSINESS, 1995

2. Disciplined

> We have this investment discipline of waiting for a fat pitch. If I was offered the chance to go into business where people would measure me against benchmarks, force me to be fully invested, crawl around looking over my shoulder, etc., I would hate it. I would regard it as putting me into shackles.
>
> —CHARLIE MUNGER, BERKSHIRE ANNUAL MEETING, 2003

> We both insist on a lot of time being available almost every day to just sit and think. That is very uncommon in American business. We

> read and think. So Warren and I do more reading and thinking and less doing than most people in business.
>
> —CHARLIE MUNGER, *KIPLINGER*, 2005

> You need patience, discipline, and an ability to take losses and adversity without going crazy.
>
> —CHARLIE MUNGER, *KIPLINGER*, 2005

> We've got great flexibility and a certain discipline in terms of not doing some foolish thing just to be active—discipline in avoiding just doing any damn thing just because you can't stand inactivity.
>
> —CHARLIE MUNGER, WESCO ANNUAL MEETING, 2000

> I think it's possible for a great many people to live a life like that where there isn't much risk of disaster and where they're virtually sure to get ahead a reasonable amount. It takes a lot of judgment, a lot of discipline, and an absence of hyperactivity. By this method, I think most intelligent people can take a lot of risk out of life.
>
> —CHARLIE MUNGER, WESCO ANNUAL MEETING, 2002

Being a Graham value investor requires discipline. It is so much easier emotionally to follow the crowd than to be a contrarian. In addition, many investors find it very difficult to do nothing. People tend to think there is a bonus for activity in investing, when there most certainly is not. Fighting this tendency can result in a big payoff because there is a penalty on being overactive due to the associated taxes, fees, and expenses.

Robert Hagstrom wrote in *The Warren Buffett Way:* "The difference between Warren Buffett and most investors has more to do with discipline than just about any other quality."[2] The same thing can be said about Munger, and there is no question that it is a trained response that will atrophy if you don't work on it. Howard Marks agreed on the importance of discipline:

Only a strong sense of value will give you the discipline needed to take profits on a highly appreciated asset that everyone thinks will rise nonstop, or the guts to hold and average down in a crisis even as prices go lower every day. Of course, for your efforts in these regards to be profitable, your estimate of value has to be on target.

—HOWARD MARKS, *THE MOST IMPORTANT THING*, 2011

Looking for signs of genuine discipline in others can be helpful in making wise decisions. For example, if you visit a money management firm that claims to be a Graham value investor and you cannot tell whether the market is open or closed, that is a good sign. Speculators correlate activity with productivity or success, whereas Graham value investors correlate disciplined inactivity with success.

3. Calm but Courageous and Decisive

I think there's something to be said for developing the disposition to own stocks without fretting.

—CHARLIE MUNGER, BERKSHIRE ANNUAL MEETING, 2003

We fret way earlier than other people. We left a lot of money on the table through early fretting. It's the way we are—you'll just have to live with it.

—CHARLIE MUNGER, WESCO ANNUAL MEETING, 2001

If you're not willing to react with equanimity to a market price decline of 50 percent two or three times a century, you're not fit to be a common shareholder and you deserve the mediocre result you're going to get compared to the people who do have the temperament, who can be more philosophical about these market fluctuations.

—CHARLIE MUNGER, BBC INTERVIEW, 2010

> If you want to get rich, you'll need a few decent ideas where you really know what you're doing. Then you've got to have the courage to stick with them and take the ups and downs. Not very complicated, and it's very old-fashioned.
>
> —CHARLIE MUNGER, *DAILY JOURNAL* MEETING, 2013

> You will get a few opportunities to profit from finding underpricing. There are actually people out there who don't price everything as high as the market will easily stand. And once you figure that out, it's like finding money in the street—if you have the courage of your convictions.
>
> —CHARLIE MUNGER, USC BUSINESS SCHOOL, 1994

> It's amazing how fast Berkshire acts when we find opportunity. You can't be timid—and that applies to all of life.
>
> —CHARLIE MUNGER, WESCO ANNUAL MEETING, 2011

Courage is an essential part of success in the Graham value investing system. If you are trying to outperform the market, mathematics dictates that you must deviate from the view of the crowd. For most people, being a contrarian requires courage. If you do not want to be courageous or do not believe you have the ability to be courageous under pressure, you should buy a portfolio of low-fee index funds and exchange-traded funds. To profit from courage, you often must have some cash on hand. Having that cash available when the crisis hits also requires courage because it's hard to sit on cash when markets are rising. The human urge to avoid missing out is a powerful one that can drive investors into the deadly grip of a stock market bubble.

If you are a Graham value investor, the best times for you are the worst times for other investors and speculators. John Templeton put it this way: "To buy when others are despondently selling and to sell when others are euphorically buying takes the greatest courage but provides the greatest profit."[3]

Market returns will always be lumpy for any investor, especially in the stock market. Drops in the prices of stocks are inevitable, and it is precisely then that people tend to panic and want to sell. Munger has experienced this several times in his lifetime, so he is not guessing on this point.

Munger suggests that investors be patient while at the same time being aggressive and decisive when the right opportunity is located. He believes that an investor has an advantage over many professionals in this way. Although professionals may have better and more current information about a given investment, they are under huge pressure to *do something* even if the best thing to do is nothing. As an example of this attribute in action, during the first quarter of 2009, when most everyone was still panicking from the financial crisis, Munger took the excess cash available in the accounts of the *Daily Journal* and plowed it into bank stocks. His timing was excellent. He had waited patiently for the right opportunity to arise and, when he saw what he wanted, he acted decisively and aggressively.

> We just put the money in. It didn't take any novel thought. It was a once-in-40-year opportunity. You have to strike the right balance between competency or knowledge on the one hand and gumption on the other. Too much competency and no gumption is no good. And if you don't know your circle of competence, then too much gumption will get you killed. But the more you know the limits to your knowledge, the more valuable gumption is. For most professional money managers, if you've got four children to put through college and you're earning $400,000 or $1 million or whatever, the last thing in the world you would want to be worried about is having gumption. You care about survival, and the way you survive is just not doing anything that might make you stand out.
>
> —CHARLIE MUNGER, JASON ZWEIG INTERVIEW, 2014

4. Reasonably Intelligent but Not Misled by Their High IQs

A lot of people with high IQs are terrible investors because they've got terrible temperaments.

—CHARLIE MUNGER, *KIPLINGER*, 2005

You need to have a passionate interest in why things are happening. That cast of mind, kept over long periods, gradually improves your ability to focus on reality. If you don't have the cast of mind, you're destined for failure even if you have a high IQ.

—CHARLIE MUNGER, BERKSHIRE ANNUAL MEETING, 2002

Very-high-IQ people can be completely useless—and many of them are.

—CHARLIE MUNGER, WESCO ANNUAL MEETING, 2010

Having a better-than-average intelligence is a precondition to being a successful active investor. Buffett has suggested that an IQ of least 125 is needed. However, Buffett has also said: "If you have more than 120 or 130 IQ points, you can afford to give the rest away. You don't need extraordinary intelligence to succeed as an investor."[4] Of course, an IQ of 125 is above average, so a certain amount of intelligence is needed. An old joke about Albert Einstein illustrates the relationship between IQ and investing: Einstein passed away and went to heaven, where he was informed that his room was not yet ready. He was told by an angel who was responsible for new arrivals: "I hope you will not mind staying for a while in a dormitory. I am sorry, but it is the best we can do right now."

The angel escorted Einstein to meet his roommates, saying, "This is your first roommate. She has an IQ of 180!"

"That's wonderful!" exclaimed Einstein. "We can discuss mathematics!"

The angel then said, "Here is your second roommate. His IQ is 150!"

"Why, that's wonderful," responded Einstein. "We can discuss physics!"

The angel finally said, "Here is your third roommate. His IQ is 100!"

"That's wonderful!" said Einstein. "Where do you think interest rates are headed?"

Smart people are not exempt from making mistakes. Unfortunately, all too often a very high IQ and market-beating investing results are inversely correlated. In other words, beyond a certain point, greater intelligence can actually be a problem. The smarter you think you are, the more you may get into trouble doing things like trying to predict things that are not predictable. Due to overconfidence, a person with a high IQ can actually make more mistakes that someone whose IQ is 30 points lower. Thinking that your IQ is a bit lower than it actually is may actually improve your investing performance.

The unfortunate truth is that intelligence and experience in one domain do not necessarily translate to another domain. More importantly, IQ tests do not assess whether a person is rational. Someone can have a very high IQ and yet not be very rational. A high-IQ individual may also not have well-developed skills, such as judgment and decision making. For these reasons, a high-IQ person outside their circle of competence is often an easy mark for the experienced promoter or compliance professional. Doctors and lawyers are favorite targets of scam promoters for this reason. For example, being wise about heart disease or estate planning does not make you wise about investing. While it is overconfidence and not high IQ which results in poor investing results, high IQ may lead to overconfidence. By being careful about things, like staying inside a circle of competence, high IQ can remain a big positive for an investor, as it is for Munger.

5. Honest

How you behave in one place will help in surprising ways later.

—CHARLIE MUNGER, *DAMN RIGHT,* 2000

Generally speaking, where Berkshire has the power, we try to be more than fair to the minority who don't have the power and who depend on us. You can say, "Aren't they wonderful, moral people?" I'm not sure we get credit for a lot of morality because we early knew how advantageous that would be to get a reputation for doing the right thing and it's worked out well for us. And my friend Peter Kaufman said, "If the rascals really knew how well honor worked, they would come to it." It really has worked well. People make contracts with Berkshire all the time because they trust us to behave well where we have the power and they don't. There's an old expression on this subject, which is really an expression on moral theory: "How nice it is to have a tyrant's strength and how wrong it is to use it like a tyrant." It's such a simple idea but it's a correct idea.

—CHARLIE MUNGER, BERKSHIRE ANNUAL MEETING, 2011

We believe there should be a huge area between everything you should do and everything you can do without getting into legal trouble. I don't think you should come anywhere near that line.

—CHARLIE MUNGER, WESCO ANNUAL MEETING, 2004

More often we've made extra money out of morality. Ben Franklin was right for us. He didn't say honesty was the best morals, he said that it was the best policy.

—CHARLIE MUNGER, WESCO ANNUAL MEETING, 2004

You ought to have an internal compass. So there should be all kinds of things you won't do even though they're perfectly legal. That's the way we try to operate.

—CHARLIE MUNGER, WESCO ANNUAL MEETING, 2004

Character matters greatly in investing and in life. Munger believes honesty is not only the right thing to do morally, but it is the approach that will produce the greatest financial return. When people in business together trust each other because they are honest, the efficiency that results from that trust improves the financial returns of the business. Munger also says that it is important to stay a safe distance away from anything illegal, dishonest, or immoral. Walking a tightrope on the razor's edge of something like honesty is unwise. On the subject of teaching honesty, Munger believes that real-life examples are often the best approach. The personal example that most guides Munger is that of his idol Benjamin Franklin:

> There's no reason to look only for living models. . . . Some of the very best models have been dead for a long time.
>
> —CHARLIE MUNGER, BERKSHIRE ANNUAL MEETING, 2000

6. Confident and Nonideological

> Develop correct confidence in your judgment.
>
> —CHARLIE MUNGER, WESCO ANNUAL MEETING, 2002

> I have a black belt in chutzpah. I was born with it.
>
> —CHARLIE MUNGER, UNIVERSITY OF CALIFORNIA, SANTA BARBARA, 2003

> The ethos of not fooling yourself is one of the best you could possibly have. It's powerful because it's so rare.
>
> —CHARLIE MUNGER, WESCO ANNUAL MEETING, 2002

Munger proves that it is possible to be confident about your beliefs and skills and still be very focused on your own potential fallibility. By being aware of your own limitations, keeping important decisions inside your circle of competence, and avoiding decisions that are too hard, it is reasonable to feel more confident in your abilities. Genuine confidence is as valuable as false confidence is dangerous. There is a huge value in knowing the difference between these two types of confidence. Finance writer Morgan Housel absolutely nailed it when he wrote, "There's a strong correlation between knowledge and humility." Humility is at the core of concepts like the circle of competence and always searching for evidence that disproves what you or others may assert. You can have a black belt in chutzpah and yet be rubbing your own nose in your own mistakes. People who are genuinely humble will make fewer mistakes. Munger has strong views about the dangers of being too ideological. He has said that heavy ideology can be one of the most dysfunctional extreme disorders.

> If you get a lot of heavy ideology young and then you start expressing it, you are locking your brain into a very unfortunate pattern. And you are going to distort your general cognition.
>
> —CHARLIE MUNGER, WESCO ANNUAL MEETING, 1998

The principal problem with ideology is that you stop thinking when it comes to hard issues. Munger believes in regularly taking your best ideas, tearing them down, and looking for flaws as a means of improving yourself, which is hard to do if you are an ideologue.

7. Long-Term Oriented

> Our system will work better in the long term.
>
> —CHARLIE MUNGER, BERKSHIRE ANNUAL MEETING, 2006

> Almost all good businesses engage in "pain today, gain tomorrow" activities.
>
> —CHARLIE MUNGER, BERKSHIRE ANNUAL MEETING, 2001

Humans evolved in an environment in which thinking about more than getting through the day or even to the next meal was not a valuable use of time. People today, who live in a very different environment, have a hard time with deferred gratification. James Montier described the problem well here:

> The penultimate hurdle is myopia (or "hyperbolic discounting," if you happen to be a geek). This reflects the idea that consequences, which occur at a later date, tend to have much less bearing on our choices the further into the future they fall. This can be summed up as, "Eat, drink and be merry, for tomorrow we may die." Of course, this ignores the fact that on any given day we are roughly 26,000 times more likely to be wrong than right with respect to making it to tomorrow. Or, if you prefer, this myopic bias can be summed up by Saint Augustine's plea: "Lord, make me chaste, but not yet."
>
> —JAMES MONTIER, *Q FINANCE*, 2009

Munger has recognized that it is hard to think on a long-term basis when you are just getting started or are starting over. For this reason, he said once that accumulating "the first $100,000 is a bitch."[5] That is reason enough to work hard to assemble a basic financial cushion. Not only is it not fun, it is a handicap to live on the edge of financial ruin.

In the long term, the power of compounding becomes ever more evident. Unfortunately, understanding the power of compounding is not a natural state for the human race; however, it is a critical task.

> Understanding both the power of compound interest and the difficulty of getting it is the heart and soul of understanding a lot of things.
>
> —CHARLIE MUNGER, *POOR CHARLIE'S ALMANACK*, 2005

Many things that are not directly financial will compound. Skills, relationships, and other aspects of life can compound and benefit a person who invests time and money wisely to cultivate these things.

8. Passionate

> What matters most: passion or competence that was born in? Berkshire is full of people who have a peculiar passion for their own business. I would argue passion is more important than brain power.
>
> —CHARLIE MUNGER, BERKSHIRE ANNUAL MEETING, 2003

As for the importance of passion in determining success in investing, business, or life in general, if you do not know about the link between passion and success, you have not been paying attention. People who are passionate tend to work harder and invest more in achieving their goals. Passionate people also read and think more. Passionate people tend to have an informational edge over others who are not as passionate. For these reasons and others, if you are playing a zero-sum game with people who are passionate and you are not, the odds that you will be a success drop substantially. One trick related to passion is that you are not likely to be passionate about something you do not understand. Often, the level of passion you will have for a topic will grow over time. The more you know about some topics, the more passionate you will get. Only becoming passionate about things that create that feeling immediately is a big mistake. Some of the best passions in life grow on you in a nonlinear way after a slow start.

9. Studious

> Learning from other people's mistakes is much more pleasant.
>
> —CHARLIE MUNGER, BERKSHIRE ANNUAL MEETING, 2012

> In my whole life, I have known no wise people (over a broad subject matter area) who didn't read all the time—none, zero. You'd be amazed at how much Warren reads, at how much I read.
>
> —CHARLIE MUNGER, BERKSHIRE ANNUAL MEETING, 2004

> Develop into a lifelong self-learner through voracious reading; cultivate curiosity and strive to become a little wiser every day.
>
> —CHARLIE MUNGER, *POOR CHARLIE'S ALMANACK*, 2005

> You gotta work where you're turned on.
>
> —CHARLIE MUNGER, BERKSHIRE ANNUAL MEETING, 2013

> The main contribution of [buying See's Candies] was ignorance removal. If it weren't . . . good at removing ignorance, we'd be nothing today. We were pretty damn stupid when we bought See's—just a little less stupid enough to buy it. The best thing about Berkshire is that we have removed a lot of ignorance. The nice thing is we still have a lot more ignorance left. . . . Another trick is scrambling out of your mistakes, which is enormously useful. We have a sure-to-fail department store. A trading stamp business sure to fold and a textile mill. Out of that comes Berkshire. Think about how we would have done if we had a better start.
>
> —CHARLIE MUNGER, BERKSHIRE ANNUAL MEETING, 2014

Munger is a believer in the investment approaches and ideas of Philip Fisher. Fisher was a successful investor based in California who wrote an influential book entitled *Common Stocks and Uncommon Profits*, first published in 1958. One of these ideas is that the successful investor is usually inherently interested in business problems. It is precisely for this reason that Ben Graham said that the best approach to investing is to be businesslike. The idea is that, in order to understand the stock, you must understand that the business is fundamental to the Graham value investing system. For this reason, investors like Fisher and Munger developed a "scuttlebutt" network of people who can help them to learn more about a business. What they inevitably find is that people involved in an industry will talk freely about their competitors as long as they believe they will not be quoted. Buffett uses the same approach:

> I would go out and talk to customers, suppliers, and maybe ex-employees in some cases. Everybody. Every time I was interested in an industry, say it was coal, I would go around and see every coal company. I would ask every CEO, "If you could only buy stock in one company that was not your own, which one would it be and why?" You piece those things together, you learn about the business after a while.
>
> —WARREN BUFFET, UNIVERSITY OF FLORIDA, 1998

Life is a lot more pleasant when you let other people make most of the big mistakes. After all, you will make enough mistakes all by yourself. Carefully learning from the mistakes of others is a way to accelerate the learning process. Nothing vicariously exposes you to more mistakes committed by others than reading.

10. Collegial

> Even Einstein didn't work in isolation. But he never went to large conferences. Any human being needs conversational colleagues.
>
> —CHARLIE MUNGER, WESCO ANNUAL MEETING, 2010

> I hardly know anybody who's done very well in life in terms of cognition that doesn't have somebody trusted to talk to. Einstein would not have been able to do what he did without people to talk to. Didn't need many but he needed some. You organize your own thoughts as you try and convince other people. It's a very necessary part of operations. If you had some hermit sitting on a mountain, he wouldn't do very well.
>
> —CHARLIE MUNGER, CNBC INTERVIEW, 2014

One great way to avoid mistakes and possibly improve your odds of success is to have someone you can run your decisions by. Buffett and Munger have the ability to do that for each other, and that approach has proven to be invaluable. Buffett calls his partner "The Abominable No-Man" because his answer on a given investment is so often "no." While you may not have a single investing partner like Munger as your colleague, having a diverse group of experienced people who you trust can be invaluable. Buffett noted in his 2013 shareholder letter that he took a massive loss because he did not run a major purchase by Munger. Buffett said the experience was painful enough that hopefully he would not do that ever again. Buffett also suggested at the same shareholder meeting that the next Berkshire CEO have a colleague (or colleagues) like Munger. Finding colleagues who can help you in life is not something that happens naturally without effort. People seldom volunteer to be colleagues, just as they do not volunteer to be mentors.

11. Sound Temperament

> Having a certain kind of temperament is more important than brains. You need to keep raw irrational emotion under control.
>
> —CHARLIE MUNGER, *KIPLINGER*, 2005

> Warren and I aren't prodigies. We can't play chess blindfolded or be concert pianists. But the results are prodigious, because we have a temperamental advantage that more than compensates for a lack of IQ points.
>
> —CHARLIE MUNGER, JASON ZWEIG INTERVIEW, 2014

How a person responds emotionally to events and other aspects of life is more important than intelligence for a Graham value investor. This emotional response to life's ups and downs, often referred to by Munger as *temperament*, will vary greatly from investor to investor. Investors who otherwise follow the Graham value investing system will often fail if they do not have a temperament that is suitable for investing. How suited a person will be in terms of temperament is a product of a combination of their natural abilities and how much they have trained themselves to improve on that baseline. Buffett put it this way: "Independent thinking, emotional stability, and a keen understanding of both human and institutional behavior are vital to long-term investment success."[6] The best investors are those who have a temperament that is calm and rational.

Some people simply do not have a temperament that is suitable for investing. No amount of training will fix that problem. Yes, there are a few people who seem to be born with a set of qualities that makes them born to use this system, but even they must work constantly throughout their lives to keep from falling prey to certain dysfunctional aspects of their temperament. For most everyone else, only continual hard work and persistence will make them into a sound Graham value investor. As is the case for many aspects of the human condition, one person's strength is often a flip side of what may create a weakness for that same person. Everyone has aspects of their life that may expose them to mistakes based on emotions and psychological errors. Seth Karman put it this way in his book *Margin of Safety*: "Unsuccessful investors are dominated by emotion. Rather than responding coolly and rationally to market fluctuations, they respond emotionally with greed and fear."[7]

Munger believes that a given investor's degree of success will be determined by how well he or she controls the dysfunctional urges that can overcome other investors. As has been noted previously, it is not possible for everyone to outperform the market. For better or worse, mistakes by other investors are the source of a Graham value investor's opportunity. One very important new approach to the Graham value investing system involves using computers and software to take human emotions completely out of the process. These machine-learning systems identify patterns consistent with Graham's value investing principles shared by companies that outperform the market. Because the process happens automatically via computer algorithms, human emotions can be removed from the stock selection process. While machine learning is not used by Buffett or Munger, it is completely consistent with their principles. Software is revolutionizing every industry, and it would be a mistake to assume that this will not be the case with investing.

Arguably the best way to sort out whether you have the right temperament for the Graham value investing system is to keep a careful written record of your investment decisions. This record-keeping will help you avoid falling prey to psychological denial. If you review your record of investing performance, you might realize that you are better off as an index investor. If you are not capable of keeping your head when all of the people around you (including Mr. Market) are losing theirs, you may not have the right temperament for the Graham value investing system. Reaching the conclusion that you are not cut out to be a Graham value investor is not a tragedy. In contrast, trying to be an active investor when you have the wrong temperament is almost certain to be a tragedy.

12. Frugal

> We don't have an isolated group [managers] surrounded by servants. Berkshire's headquarters is a tiny little suite.
>
> —CHARLIE MUNGER, WESCO ANNUAL MEETING, 2004

> If you take the money invested in common stocks, and then subtract the 2 percent per year that goes out in investment management costs and fractional trading costs, that's more than companies pay in dividends. . . .This would fit very well into *Alice in Wonderland*; pay dividends of X and pay the same amount to investment managers and advisors.
>
> —CHARLIE MUNGER, WESCO ANNUAL MEETING, 2004

> Mozart . . . overspent his income his entire life—that will make you miserable.
>
> —CHARLIE MUNGER, WESCO ANNUAL MEETING, 2007

Like his idol Benjamin Franklin and his partner Buffett, Munger is relatively frugal given his wealth, especially when it comes to operating and investment expenses. In addition to the axiom "a penny saved is two pence dear,"[8] Benjamin Franklin wrote: "The way to wealth is as plain as the way to market. It depends chiefly on two words, industry and frugality: that is, waste neither time nor money, but make the best use of both. Without industry and frugality nothing will do, and with them, everything."[9] Other Graham value investors have a similar focus on frugality. Walter Schloss was famous for running his investment firm out of a single room leased from another investment firm. I suspect that some of the frugality that can be seen in Graham value investors springs from their understanding of opportunity cost and the power of compounding. They naturally compare the value of consumption today with the value of greater consumptions tomorrow, which causes them to be frugal.

13. Risk Averse

> Using [a stock's] volatility as a measure of risk is nuts. Risk to us is 1) the risk of permanent loss of capital, or 2) the risk of inadequate return. Some great businesses have very volatile returns—for example, See's Candies usually loses money in two quarters of each year—and some terrible businesses can have steady results.
>
> —CHARLIE MUNGER, BERKSHIRE ANNUAL MEETING, 1997

> This is an amazingly sound place. We are more disaster-resistant than most other places. We haven't pushed it as hard as other people would have pushed it. I don't want to go back to *Go* [like in a game of Monopoly]. I've been to *Go*. . . . A lot of our shareholders have a majority of their net worth in Berkshire, and they don't want to go back to *Go* either.
>
> —CHARLIE MUNGER, WESCO ANNUAL MEETING, 2001

> You can easily see how risk-averse Berkshire is. In the first place, we try and behave in such a way that no rational person is going to worry about our credit. And after we have done that, we also behave in such a way that if the world suddenly didn't like our credit, we wouldn't even notice it for months, because we have so much liquidity. That double layering of protection against risk is as natural as breathing around Berkshire. It's just part of the culture.
>
> —CHARLIE MUNGER, BERKSHIRE ANNUAL MEETING, 2008

As the quotes above make clear, Munger strongly believes risk cannot be fully measured by the volatility of investment prices in markets, as some people claim. Volatility is certainly one type of risk. For example, if you are retiring or have tuition bills to pay at a certain time, volatility is one type of risk you must face, but it is not the only risk. Why do investment managers try to equate risk with volatility rather than just considering it as one important type of risk? There are many money managers who want you to believe that volatility is equal to risk because volatility is a major risk for them because, if stocks drop in price, investors will flee from their services. These money managers also love equating risk with volatility because it gives investors the impression that risk can be precisely quantified, which helps justify their fees. Risk cannot be fully expressed as a number. Why do academics also try to equate risk with volatility? Munger believes this happens because (1) it helps make their mathematics beautiful, even though it has little tie to reality, and (2) it can lead to attractive consulting contracts with money management firms. People like Nassim Taleb have written books that chronicle how flawed risk management has resulted in crisis after crisis. One story sometimes told by investors goes like this: A surgeon, an accountant, and a risk manager at a bank are debating whose profession goes back the furthest. The surgeon says, "God made Eve out of Adam's rib. Obviously surgery came first."

The accountant disagreed and said, "Before that, God created the universe by bringing order out of chaos. That's accounting."

The risk manager then chimed in. "I've got you both beat," she says. "Answer me this. Who created the chaos?"

For the best essay on the proper definition of risk, it's a good idea to read Buffett's 1993 Berkshire shareholder's letter. Buffett pointed out that risk comes from not knowing what you're doing. Risk is something an investor should retire rather than "dial up." Buffett illustrated the best way to deal with risk with a story:

> Every two years I'm part of an informal group that gathers to have fun and explore a few subjects. Last September, meeting at Bishop's Lodge in Santa Fe, we asked [Ike Friedman, Borsheim's managing Genius] to come by and educate us on jewels and the jewelry business. Ike decided to dazzle the group, so he brought from Omaha about $20 million of particularly fancy merchandise. I was somewhat apprehensive—Bishop's Lodge is no Fort Knox—and I mentioned my concern to Ike at our opening party the evening before his presentation. Ike took me aside. "See that safe?" he said. "This afternoon we changed the combination and now even the hotel management doesn't know what it is." I breathed easier. Ike went on: "See those two big fellows with guns on their hips? They'll be guarding the safe all night." I now was ready to rejoin the party. But Ike leaned closer: "And besides, Warren," he confided, "the jewels aren't in the safe."
>
> —WARREN BUFFETT, 1989 BERKSHIRE SHAREHOLDER LETTER, 1990

6

THE SEVEN VARIABLES IN THE GRAHAM VALUE INVESTING SYSTEM

NOW THAT THE fundamental principles of the Graham value investing system have been discussed, it is time to discuss how investors can differ in their styles and still remain Graham value investors. You will recall that in this book's Principles, Right Stuff, and Variables framework, aspects of a Graham value investor's style that differ are called *variables*.

First Variable: Determining the Appropriate Intrinsic Value of a Business

The definition of intrinsic value in the Owner's Manual of Berkshire Hathaway is as follows:

> Intrinsic value can be defined simply: It's the discounted value of the cash that can be taken out of a business during its remaining life. The calculation of intrinsic value, though, is not so simple. As our definition suggests, intrinsic value is an estimate rather than a

> precise figure, and it's additionally an estimate that must be changed if interest rates move or forecasts of future cash flows are revised.
>
> —WARREN BUFFETT, BERKSHIRE HATHAWAY OWNER'S MANUAL, 2014

Because the cash that can flow from a business is not an annuity and instead is based on a number of fundamental factors that are impossible to predict with certainty, determining the value of a business is an art and not a science. Almost every investor will have a slightly different way of determining the intrinsic value of a business, and there is nothing inherently wrong with that fact. For this reason, it is best to think about intrinsic value as falling within a range rather than an exact figure.

Some businesses have an intrinsic value that is relatively easy to calculate, whereas other businesses have an intrinsic value that value investors have little idea how to calculate. Munger does not even try to value businesses in every possible case:

> We have no system for estimating the correct value of all businesses. We put almost all in the "too hard" pile and sift through a few easy ones.
>
> —CHARLIE MUNGER, BERKSHIRE ANNUAL MEETING, 2007

In an ideal situation, the process of determining the intrinsic valuation of a business is easy enough that Munger can do that valuation in his head. While people of more ordinary intelligence may need to use a calculator to do the same mathematics, Munger's point about a desire for simplicity and an obvious result remains true for any Graham value investor. If Munger determines that the valuation of the business is too hard, he simply says, "I pass." This is such a powerful and underutilized idea. To use a baseball analogy, Munger and Buffett love the fact that they are not required to swing the bat as an investor in response to every pitch.

The tendency of many people who are overconfident is just the reverse of Munger's use of a "too hard" pile. In other words, people with a high IQ often relish the opportunity to solve hard valuation problems, thinking that they will be rewarded for having such ample mental skill with a higher return. The reality is that, in trying to solve hard problems, emotional and psychological problems cause the losses rather than a lack of intelligence. Hard problems are hard problems, pregnant with opportunities to make mistakes.

Determining the value of a business is best done and is most reliable when the process is simple. Even in a case where the process is relatively simple, a Graham value investor must remember that the valuation process is inherently imprecise. An imprecise value is perfectly acceptable to a value investor because the Graham value investor is looking for a margin of safety that is so substantial that precise calculation is unnecessary. A good analogy is a waiter trying to decide whether a customer is above the legal drinking age. There are certain restaurant patrons who are obviously older than the legal drinking age, just as there are certain businesses with an intrinsic value that obviously provides the necessary margin of safety.

Buffett and Munger admit they do not have exactly the same definition of intrinsic value. Buffett believes:

> Intrinsic value is terribly important but very fuzzy. Two people looking at the same set of facts, moreover—and this would apply even to Charlie and me—will almost inevitably come up with at least slightly different intrinsic value figures.
>
> —WARREN BUFFETT, BERKSHIRE ANNUAL MEETING, 2003

The definition is fuzzy enough that really smart and experienced investors can do the math in their head.

> Warren talks about these discounted cash flows. I've never seen him do one.
>
> —CHARLIE MUNGER, *WARREN BUFFET SPEAKS*, 2007

In his 1994 Berkshire chairman's letter, Buffett wrote that "intrinsic value [is] a number that is impossible to pinpoint but essential to estimate.... Despite its fuzziness, however, intrinsic value is all-important and is the only logical way to evaluate the relative attractiveness of investments and businesses."[1] While the views and approaches to valuation may vary in some detail, they are generally consistent. Valuation is not a process in which a Graham value investor makes stuff up as he or she goes along. In the view of Michael Price: "Intrinsic value is what a businessman would pay for total control of the business with full due diligence and a big bank line. The biggest indicator to me is where the fully controlled position trades, not where the market trades it or where the stock trades relative to comparable [businesses]."[2]

There are some businesses with certain qualities that Munger will not touch with a ten-foot pole:

> There are two kinds of businesses: The first earns 12 percent, and you can take it out at the end of the year. The second earns 12 percent, but all the excess cash must be reinvested—there's never any cash. It reminds me of the guy who looks at all of his equipment and says, "There's all of my profit." We hate that kind of business.
>
> —CHARLIE MUNGER, BERKSHIRE ANNUAL MEETING, 2003

When Munger and Buffett value a business, they use what they call *owner's earnings* as the starting point. Owner's earnings can be defined as: Net income + Depreciation + Depletion + Amortization − Capital expenditure − Additional working capital. Berkshire uses the owner's earnings figure in this process to take into account capital expenditures that will be necessary to maintain the business's return on equity. A more complete explanation of an owner's earnings calculation is provided in the section of this book called Berkshire Math.

Owner's earnings is not a typical valuation metric. Other Graham value investors may use different metrics, like earnings before interest and taxes (EBIT), in calculating value. For example, in *The Little Book that Beats the Market*, Greenblatt says that he views the depreciation part of EBIT as a proxy for capital expenditures and seems to imply that replacing depreciation with capital expenditure would be a better approach.

Buffett has views on the importance of growth in determining the value of a business, which echo Munger's approach:

> Growth is always a component in the calculation of value, constituting a variable whose importance can range from negligible to enormous and whose impact can be negative as well as positive. . . . Growth benefits investors only when the business in point can invest at incremental returns that are enticing – in other words, only when each dollar used to finance the growth creates over a dollar of long-term market value. In the case of a low-return business requiring incremental funds, growth hurts the investor.
>
> —WARREN BUFFETT, 1992 BERKSHIRE SHAREHOLDER LETTER, 1993

It is more important that the definition of intrinsic value stay consistent in the mind of a given investor than that the calculation be the same as every other Graham value investor. As will be explained, intrinsic value is a reference point in the final analysis for investors as they patiently watch the price of an investment gyrate up and down in price over time. In doing a valuation analysis, Graham value investors like Munger are very conservative.

Second Variable: Determining the Appropriate Margin of Safety

Margin of safety is a simple idea that is applied in different ways by different investors. Some investors like to have a margin of safety that is much larger than others. For example, one Graham value investor may require a 25 percent margin of safety, whereas another needs 40 percent. Of course, because the concept of intrinsic value itself is imprecise, the calculation of margin of safety is necessarily imprecise. Making things easier is the fact that Munger and Buffett like the amount of a margin of safety to be so big that they need not do any math other than in their heads. Of course, Buffett and Munger can do more mathematics in their heads than an average person can do on a calculator, but the point remains. Munger wants the math involved in evaluating an investment to be simple, overpoweringly clear, and positive. Bill Gates has commented on this point:

> Being good with numbers doesn't necessarily correlate with being a good investor. Warren doesn't outperform other investors because he computes odds better. That's not it at all. Warren never makes an investment where the difference between doing it and not doing it relies on the second digit of computation. He doesn't invest—take a swing of the bat—unless the opportunity appears unbelievably good.
>
> —BILL GATES, *FORTUNE*, 1996

Many people make the mistake of assuming that buying a quality company ensures safety. A given company may be a quality company with an attractive business, but that alone is not enough because the price you pay for a share of stock matters. A company like Facebook, Nike, or even Berkshire may be an important company with lots of revenue and profit, but its business is not worth an infinite price. Howard Marks put it best:

> Most investors think quality, as opposed to price, is the determinant of whether something's risky. But high quality assets can be risky, and low quality assets can be safe. It's just a matter of the price paid for them. . . . Elevated popular opinion, then, isn't just the source of low return potential, but also of high risk.
>
> —HOWARD MARKS, *THE MOST IMPORTANT THING*, 2011

Similarly, just because the price of a share of stock in a company is beaten down from formerly high levels does not make it safe to buy. In other words, that a given company is way off its value of a few years ago does not necessarily make the purchase of the stock safe in terms of a margin of safety.

Munger talked once about the concept of margin of safety in describing Buffett's mentor Benjamin Graham in this way:

> Graham had this concept of value to a private owner—what the whole enterprise would sell for if it were available. And that was calculable in many cases. Then, if you could take the stock price and multiply it by the number of shares and get something that was one third or less of sellout value, he would say that you've got a lot of edge going for you. Even with an elderly alcoholic running a stodgy business, this significant excess of real value per share working for you means that all kinds of good things can happen to you. You had a huge margin of safety—as he put it—by having this big excess value going for you.
>
> —CHARLIE MUNGER, UNIVERSITY OF SOUTHERN CALIFORNIA (USC) BUSINESS SCHOOL, 1994

While the calculations of the intrinsic value and margin of safety are imprecise and fuzzy, they remain critical tasks in the Graham value investing system. As James Montier wrote:

> Valuation is the closest thing to the law of gravity that we have in finance. It's the primary determinant of long-term returns. However, the objective of investment (in general) is not to buy at fair value, but to purchase with a margin of safety. This reflects that any estimate of fair value is just that: an estimate, not a precise figure, so the margin of safety provides a much-needed cushion against errors and misfortunes. When investors violate [this principle] by investing with no margin of safety, they risk the prospect of the permanent impairment of capital.
>
> —JAMES MONTIER, *THE SEVEN IMMUTABLE LAWS OF INVESTING*, 2011

The golden rule of investing: no asset (or strategy) is so good that you should invest irrespective of the price paid.

—JAMES MONTIER, GMO LETTER, DECEMBER 2013

Third Variable: Determining the Scope of an Investor's Circle of Competence

We have to deal with things that we're capable of understanding.

—CHARLIE MUNGER, BBC INTERVIEW, 2009

We'd rather deal with what we understand. Why should we want to play a competitive game in a field where we have no advantages—maybe a disadvantage—instead of playing in a field where we have a clear advantage? Each of you will have to figure out where your talent lies. And you'll have to use your advantages. But if you try to succeed in what you're worst at, you're going to have a very lousy career. I can almost guarantee it. To do otherwise, you'd have to buy a winning lottery ticket or get very lucky somewhere else.

—CHARLIE MUNGER, STANFORD UNIVERSITY LAW SCHOOL, 1998

I don't think it's difficult to figure out competence. If you're 5'2", say no to professional basketball. Ninety-two years old, you're not going to be the romantic lead in Hollywood. At 350 pounds, you don't dance the lead in the Bolshoi ballet . . . Competency is a relative concept.

—CHARLIE MUNGER, BERKSHIRE ANNUAL MEETING, 2014

I'm really better at determining my level of incompetency and then just avoiding that. And I prefer to think that question through in reverse. We have a good batting average and that is probably because we are a little more competent than we think we are.

—CHARLIE MUNGER, CNBC INTERVIEW, 2014

Understanding the limits of your own competence is very valuable. Venture capitalist Fred Wilson put it simply: "The only way you win is by knowing what you're good at and what you're not good at, and sticking to what you're good at."[3] Munger similarly believes that investors who get outside of what he calls their circle of competence can easily find themselves in big trouble. Within his or her circle of competence, an investor has expertise and knowledge that gives them a significant advantage over the market in evaluating an investment.

The idea behind the circle of competence is so simple that it is arguably embarrassing to say it out loud: when you do not know what you're doing, it is riskier than when you do know what you're doing. What could be simpler? And yet, humans often do not act in accordance with this idea. For example, the otherwise smart doctor or dentist is easy prey for the promoter selling limited partnerships or securities in a company that makes technology for the petroleum industry.

Munger has pointed out that even one of the world's greatest investors stepped outside of his circle of competence during the Internet bubble:

> Soros couldn't bear to see others make money in the technology sector without him, and he got killed.
>
> —CHARLIE MUNGER, BERKSHIRE ANNUAL MEETING, 2000

The circle of competence approach is a form of opportunity cost analysis, says Munger:

> Warren and I only look at industries and companies which we have a core competency in. Every person has to do the same thing. You have a limited amount of time and talent and you have to allocate it smartly.
>
> —CHARLIE MUNGER, WESCO ANNUAL MEETING, 2011

The value of specialization is, of course, at work here too. Munger put it this way:

> Warren and I have skills that could easily be taught to other people. One skill is knowing the edge of your own competency. It's not a competency if you don't know the edge of it. And Warren and I are better at tuning out the standard stupidities. We've left a lot of more talented and diligent people in the dust, just by working hard at eliminating standard error.
>
> —CHARLIE MUNGER, *STANFORD LAWYER*, 2009

Munger has a range of approaches he uses to avoid mistakes. To make this point by analogy, Munger is fond of saying that he wants to know where he will die so he can intentionally never go there. His friend and investor Li Lu described one such approach:

> When Charlie thinks about things, he starts by inverting. To understand how to be happy in life Charlie will study how to make life miserable; to examine how a business becomes big and strong, Charlie first studies how businesses decline and die; most people care more about how to succeed in the stock market, Charlie is most concerned about why most have failed in the stock market.
>
> —LI LU, *CHINA ENTREPRENEUR MAGAZINE*, 2010

By adopting this approach Munger is trying hard to limit his investing to areas in which he has a significant advantage in terms of competence and not just a basic understanding. To illustrate this point, he has in the past talked about a man who had "managed to corner the market in shoe buttons—a really small market, but he had it all."[4] It is possible to earn an attractive financial return in a very limited domain like shoe buttons, although that is an extreme example of a very narrow circle of competence. The areas in which you might have a circle of competence will hopefully be significantly larger than just shoe buttons. However, if you try to expand that circle of competence too far, it can have disastrous results. Li Lu has written about how Munger has described this point to him:

> The true insights a person can get in life are still very limited, so correct decision making must necessarily be confined to your "circle of competence." A "competence" that has no defined borders cannot be called a true competence.
>
> —LI LU, *CHINA ENTREPRENEUR MAGAZINE*, 2010

Once the borders of a circle of competence are established, the challenge is to remain inside those borders. Staying within a circle of competence is obviously not rocket science in theory, but it is hard for most people to do in practice. Lapses by investors are more likely to occur when they meet a slick promoter who is highly skilled at telling stories. This is a case where emotional intelligence, which is very different than intellectual intelligence, becomes critically important. Humans love stories because they cause them to suspend disbelief. Some of the biggest frauds in financial history, like Bernie Madoff and Ken Lay, were excellent storytellers. Stories cause people to suspend disbelief, and being in that state is harmful to any person's investing process.

Too many investors confuse familiarity with competence. For example, just because a person flies on airlines a lot does not mean that he or she understands the airline industry well enough to be competent as an investor in that sector of the economy. Using Facebook a lot does not make you qualified to invest in a social media startup. If you have not gone beyond simply using a product or service and have not taken a deep dive into the business of a company, you should not invest in that company.

Among the people who know how to stay within their circle of competence are the chief executive officers of Berkshire subsidiaries. For example, Buffett once pointed to Rose Blumkin of Furniture Mart as a person who fully understands the dimensions of her capabilities:

> [If] you got about two inches outside the perimeter of her circle of competence, she didn't even talk about it. She knew exactly what she was good at, and she had no desire to kid herself about those things.
>
> —WARREN BUFFETT, *THE SNOWBALL*, 2008

Knowing the boundaries of your circle of competence is critically important. He feels that the answer should be obvious:

> If you have competence, you pretty much know its boundaries already. To ask the question [of whether you're past the boundary] is to answer it.
>
> —CHARLIE MUNGER, BERKSHIRE ANNUAL MEETING, 2002

Buffett talks about that fact that knowing where the perimeter of your circle of competence may be is far more important than the size of your circle. If you are only competent in spots and stay in those spots, you can do just fine. Munger has said on this point:

> There are a lot of things we pass on. All of you have to look for a special area of competency and focus on that.
>
> —CHARLIE MUNGER, WESCO ANNUAL MEETING, 2002

It is critical that an investor remain focused on avoiding mistakes. If someone tries to sell you something that requires decisions that are too hard, you have the option to just say no. Why would you do what is hard when you can find investments that involve easy decisions? In using a circle of competence filter, Munger is trying to invest only when he has an unfair advantage. Otherwise, he wants to do nothing (which most people find very hard to do).

> The reason we are not in high-tech businesses is that we have a special lack of aptitude in that area. And, yes—low-tech business can be plenty hard. Just try to open a restaurant and make it succeed. . . . Why should it be easy to get rich? In a competitive world, shouldn't an easy way to get rich be impossible.
>
> —CHARLIE MUNGER, WESCO MEETING, 1998

In a sector of the economy like technology, Munger and Buffett have both said they do not understand the businesses well enough to be technology investors. They don't feel like they can forecast what owners' earnings from a technology-driven business will be like even in five years, let alone for decades. Because every business uses technology, Munger and Buffett are not excluding them from their circle of competence.

Munger's reluctance to invest in the technology sector can be traced to mistakes that he made early in his life because he stepped outside of his circle of competence. Munger received his first taste of the technology business when he bought into a company that made instruments early in his investing career. His experience in that case was not good. His top scientist was hired away by a venture capitalist; then magnetic tape came along, which made the performance of the business even worse. Munger said once that the entire experience nearly made him, in his words, "go broke."

> Warren and I don't feel like we have any great advantage in the high-tech sector. In fact, we feel like we're at a big disadvantage in trying to understand the nature of technical developments in software, computer chips or what have you. So we tend to avoid that stuff, based on our personal inadequacies. Again, that is a very, very powerful idea. Every person is going to have a circle of competence. And it's going to be very hard to advance that circle. If I had to make my living as a musician—I can't even think of a level low enough to describe where I would be sorted out to if music were the measuring standard of the civilization.
>
> —CHARLIE MUNGER, USC BUSINESS SCHOOL, 1994

Munger's personal decision regarding investing in technology companies does not mean that the technology sector is not right for other people who have a circle of competence that includes technology.

Technology presents additional challenges because uncertainty is high and the speed of innovation vastly faster. Buffett has said: "Predicting the long-term economics of companies that operate in fast-changing industries is simply far beyond our perimeter."[5] An investor can cope with that difference by being careful about his or her circle of competence within technology. To know a lot about graphics chips is not necessarily to know much about wireless data, for example. To think otherwise is to tempt fate. As Clint Eastwood asked in the movie *Dirty Harry:* "You've got to ask yourself one question: 'Do I feel lucky?' Well, do ya?"

Fourth Variable: Determining How Much of Each Security to Buy

> Our investment style has been given a name—focus investing—which implies 10 holdings, not 100 or 400. Focus investing is growing somewhat, but what's really growing is the unlimited use of consultants to advise on asset allocation, to analyze other consultants, etc.
>
> —CHARLIE MUNGER, WESCO ANNUAL MEETING, 2010

In addition to complaining about consultants and their fees, Munger is saying that diversification is not an approach that is attractive to him. Some Graham value investors diversify, while others like Munger concentrate their investment portfolio. A person can adopt either concentrated or diversified portfolio strategies and still be a Graham value investor. Once he made the decision to become an active investor, Munger became a devotee of concentrating his investments. Typical of Munger's views on these issues is the following:

> [With] closet indexing . . . you're paying a manager a fortune and he has 85 percent of his assets invested parallel to the indexes. If you have such a system, you're being played for a sucker.
>
> —CHARLIE MUNGER, WESCO ANNUAL MEETING, 2005

Munger developed this philosophy in no small part by learning from the example of Phil Fisher. When it comes to diversification versus concentration, Munger believes that focus is the better answer for him:

> I always like it when someone attractive to me agrees with me, so I have fond memories of Phil Fisher. The idea that it was hard to find good investments, to concentrate in a few, seems to me to be an obviously good idea. But 98 percent of the investment world doesn't think this way.
>
> —CHARLIE MUNGER, BERKSHIRE ANNUAL MEETING, 2004

Each investor who chooses focus investing over diversification has a slightly different reason for doing so, but there is commonality on some points. Seth Klarman pointed out that it is better to know a lot about ten or fifteen companies than to know just a little about many. The number of stocks a person can realistically follow and understand the economics of the specific business better than the market is significantly less than twenty. For example, the idea that a dentist working full time in his or her profession is going to pick technology stocks better than the market, especially after fees and expenses, is unlikely. Remember the task is not just to pick a quality company, but to find a mispriced bet.

There are other Graham value investors who disagree with Munger and instead believe in diversification. Two notable examples were Ben Graham himself and Walter Schloss. Jason Zweig has pointed out that, "Even the great investment analyst Benjamin Graham urged 'adequate though not excessive diversification,' which he defined as between 10 and about 30 securities."[6] After a significant number of years had passed after the Great Depression, it was no longer possible to be widely diversified and only invest in public stocks. Some investors who seek greater diversification than Munger invest in less liquid and less frequently traded markets, like distressed debt. Of course, these less liquid and traded markets are also places where asset mispricing is more likely to occur, and rational Graham value investors can find bargains. Buffett believes that diversification is protection against not knowing what you're doing—and when it comes to investing, nearly no one knows what they are doing. The most diversified approach is to buy a portfolio of low-fee index funds and exchange-traded funds.

Munger considers one of the saddest cases in investing to be when someone thinks they are an active investor, but in reality they have invested in so many stocks that they have become "closet indexers." Investors who adopt the Berkshire system are focus investors. Munger noted:

> The Berkshire-style investors tend to be less diversified than other people. The academics have done a terrible disservice to intelligent investors by glorifying the idea of diversification. Because I just think the whole concept is literally almost insane. It emphasizes feeling good about not having your investment results depart very much from average investment results. But why would you get on the bandwagon like that if somebody didn't make you with a whip and a gun?
>
> —CHARLIE MUNGER, *KIPLINGER*, 2005

Fifth Variable: Determining When to Sell a Security

> Selling [something] when it approaches your calculation of its intrinsic value [is] hard. But if you buy a few great companies, then you can sit on your ass. That's a good thing.
>
> —CHARLIE MUNGER, BERKSHIRE ANNUAL MEETING, 2000

> We tend not to sell operating businesses. That is a lifestyle choice. We have bought well. We have a few which would be better if we sold them. But net we do better if we don't do gin rummy management, churning our portfolio. We want a reputation as not being churners and flippers. Competitive advantage is being not a churner.
>
> —CHARLIE MUNGER, WESCO ANNUAL MEETING, 2008

> To us, investing is the equivalent of going out and betting against the pari-mutuel system. We look for a horse with one chance in two of winning, and that pays three to one. In other words, we're looking for a mispriced gamble. That's what investing is, and you have to know enough to know whether the gamble is mispriced.
>
> —CHARLIE MUNGER, USC BUSINESS SCHOOL, 1994

> There are huge advantages for an individual to get into a position where you make a few great investments and just sit back and wait: you're paying less to brokers. You're listening to less nonsense. And if it works, the governmental tax system gives you an extra 1, 2 or 3 percentage points per annum compounded.
>
> —CHARLIE MUNGER, *DAMN RIGHT*, 2000

Munger is pointing out in the above quotes that Graham value investors have adopted a range of approaches to the question of when or whether to sell a given investment. Munger prefers to buy a business or a portion of a business and own it essentially forever. His preference is in no small part driven by the ability of a long-term holder of an asset to gain certain tax and other advantages. By not incurring these tax costs, transaction costs, and other fees, the compounding benefits for the investor are substantially higher. Unlike Munger, some other Graham value investors choose to sell assets when they reach something approaching their intrinsic value. There is no right answer on whether or when to sell an asset, and how a particular investor answers this question is partially a matter of temperament. However, most Graham value investors seem to prefer Munger's approach.

Sixth Variable: Determining How Much to Bet When You Find a Mispriced Asset

> It's not given to human beings to have such talent that they can just know everything about everything all the time. But it's given to

human beings who work hard at it—who look and sift the world for a mispriced bet—that they can occasionally find one.

—CHARLIE MUNGER, USC BUSINESS SCHOOL, 1994

We came to this notion of finding a mispriced bet and loading up when we were very confident that we were right.

—CHARLIE MUNGER, USC BUSINESS SCHOOL, 1994

The wise ones bet heavily when the world offers them that opportunity. They bet big when they have the odds. And the rest of the time, they don't. It's just that simple.

—CHARLIE MUNGER, USC BUSINESS SCHOOL, 1994

Playing poker in the Army and as a young lawyer honed my business skills. . . . What you have to learn is to fold early when the odds are against you, or if you have a big edge, back it heavily because you don't get a big edge often.

—CHARLIE MUNGER, *DAMN RIGHT*, 2000

The model I like—to sort of simplify the notion of what goes on in a market for common stocks—is the pari-mutuel system at the racetrack. . . . Everybody goes there and bets and the odds change based on what's bet. That's what happens in the stock market. Any damn fool can see that a horse carrying a light weight with a wonderful win rate and a good post position etc., etc., is way more likely to win than a horse with a terrible record and extra weight and so on and so on. But if you look at the odds, the bad horse pays 100 to 1, whereas the good horse pays 3 to 2. Then it's not clear which is statistically the best bet, using the mathematics of Fermat and Pascal.

—CHARLIE MUNGER, USC BUSINESS SCHOOL, 1994

By investing only within his circle of competence, Munger is trying to invest only when he has an unfair advantage. When he has an unfair advantage, which is not that often, he bets big. This means he will be less active than other investors. Munger believes that buying and selling a stock for its own sake (e.g., to stay busy) is a very bad idea. Munger's bias against what he calls investment hyperactivity is quite strong. When in doubt, his suggestion is that you do nothing.

> Around here, I would say that if our predictions have been a little better than other people's, it's because we've tried to make fewer of them.
>
> —CHARLIE MUNGER, BERKSHIRE ANNUAL MEETING, 1998

> We try and predict what individual investments will swim well in relation to the tide. And then we tend to accept the effects of the tide as those effects fall.
>
> —CHARLIE MUNGER, WESCO ANNUAL MEETING, 2001

Munger does not like situations where there is a close investment decision to make. He would certainly not invest in anything with a big downside and a small upside. One of the best ways I have ever heard the idea behind his philosophy expressed was by the famed investor Sam Zell:

> Listen, business is easy. If you've got a low downside and a big upside, you go do it. If you've got a big downside and a small upside, you run away. The only time you have any work to do is when you have a big downside and a big upside.
>
> —SAM ZELL, *NEW YORKER*, 2007

In terms of finance theory, what a smart investor is looking for is *optionality*. Nassim Taleb described what the smart investor is looking for in this way: "Payoffs [that] follow a power law type of statistical distribution, with big, near unlimited upside but because of optionality, limited downside."[7] There is a joke that illustrates the value of optionality: An investment banker and carpenter are sitting next to each other on a long flight. The investment banker asks the carpenter if she would like to play a fun game. The carpenter is tired and just wants to have a nap, so she politely declines and tries to sleep. The investment banker loudly insists that the game is a lot of fun and says, "I will ask you a question, and if you don't know the answer you must pay me only $5. Then you ask me one question, and if I don't know the answer, I will pay you $500." To keep him quiet, she agrees to play the game.

The investment banker asks the first question: "What's the distance from the earth to the Saturn?" The carpenter doesn't say a word, pulls out $5, and hands it to the investment banker.

The carpenter then asks the investment banker, "What goes up a hill with three legs and comes down with four?" She then closes her eyes again to rest.

The investment banker immediately opens his laptop computer, connects to the in-flight Wi-Fi, and searches the Internet for an answer without success. He then sends emails to all of his smart friends, who also have no answer. After two hours of searching, he finally gives up. The investment banker wakes up the carpenter and hands her $500. The carpenter takes the $500 and goes back to sleep. The investment banker is going crazy from not knowing the answer. So he wakes her up and asks, "What does go up a hill with three legs and comes down with four?"

The carpenter hands the investment banker $5 and goes back to sleep.

Seventh Variable: Determining Whether the Quality of a Business Should Be Considered

> Ben Graham had blind spots. He had too low an appreciation of the fact that some businesses were worth paying big premiums for.
>
> —CHARLIE MUNGER, *DAMN RIGHT*, 2000

Munger's approach to valuing a business is influenced in part by Ben Graham and in part by Phil Fisher. The importance of Phil Fisher to the evolution of Munger's thinking on the Graham value investing system is fundamental. For Fisher, wide diversification is essentially a form of closet indexing. He instead believed that an investor should focus on a relatively small number of stocks if he or she expects to outperform a market. Fisher preferred a holding period of almost forever; for example, he bought Motorola in 1955 and held it until 2004. Fisher also believed that a fat pitch investment opportunity is delivered rarely and only to those investors who are willing to patiently work to find them. Fisher felt that business cycles and changes in Mr. Market's attitude are inevitable. Unlike many other investors, Fisher assigned significant weight to the quality of the underlying business. For this reason, Fisher was able to outperform markets as an investor, even though he did not look for cigar-butt stocks.

An approach that incorporates the ideas of Fisher is very different from the approach of a Graham value investor like Seth Klarman. Both Munger and Seth Klarman want a margin of safety, which is a Graham value investing principle, but each investor chooses to calculate both intrinsic value and margin of safety in different ways. For Munger, the approach used by Fisher was clearly superior:

> If I'd never lived, Warren would have morphed into liking the better businesses better and being less interested in deep-value cigar butts. The supply of cigar butts was running out. . . . The natural drift was going that way without Charlie Munger. But he'd been brainwashed a little by worshiping Ben Graham and making so much money following traditional Graham methods that I may have pushed him along a little faster in the direction that he was already going.
>
> —CHARLIE MUNGER, *KIPLINGER*, 2005

> The trouble with what I call the classic Ben Graham concept is that gradually the world wised up [after enough time had passed after the Great Depression] and those real obvious bargains disappeared. . . . Ben Graham followers responded by changing the calibration on their Geiger counters. In effect, they started defining a

> bargain in a different way. And it still worked pretty well. So the Ben Graham intellectual system was a very good one.
>
> —CHARLIE MUNGER, USC BUSINESS SCHOOL, 1994

Buffett today is arguably more like Fisher than the 15 percent he once specified, but only he knows how much of my assertion is true. It was the influence of Munger that moved Buffett a considerable distance away from a pure Ben Graham approach. Their investment in See's Candies was an early example in which Berkshire paid more for a quality company. What Munger and Buffett found was that See's Candies had untapped pricing power which was able to increase its financial return in a very significant way. The two investors found after they bought See's Candies, they could regularly raise prices and customers did not seem to care. Munger calls this ability to raise prices and not cause a significant drop in sales "pricing power." Buffett said once, "More than 50 years ago, Charlie told me that it was far better to buy a wonderful business at a fair price than to buy a fair business at a wonderful price."[8] What Charlie is talking about here is the idea that a business with superior quality bought at the right price can still be a bargain purchase consistent with the principles of the Graham value investing system.

Part of the reason this shift to Fisher's approach to valuing a business happened is that the sorts of companies that Graham liked to buy started to disappear the further away the time period was from the Great Depression. The other push toward Fisher's ideas came because of the success Munger and Buffett were having in markets. Because of their consistent and persistent financial success, Berkshire must put massive amounts of cash to work every year, and finding enough cigar-butt investments at that scale is an impossible task.

Unlike more pure Graham style investors, Munger believed his investing style had to evolve.

> Grahamites . . . realized that some company that was selling at two or three times book value could still be a hell of a bargain because of momentums implicit in its position, sometimes combined with an

> unusual managerial skill plainly present in some individual or other, or some system or other. And once we'd gotten over the hurdle of recognizing that a thing could be a bargain based on quantitative measures that would have horrified Graham, we started thinking about better businesses.
>
> —CHARLIE MUNGER, USC BUSINESS SCHOOL, 1994

For Munger, not considering the quality of the underlying business when buying an asset is far too limiting.

> The investment game always involves considering both quality and price, and the trick is to get more quality than you pay for in price. It's just that simple.
>
> —CHARLIE MUNGER, *DAMN RIGHT*, 2000

> We've really made the money out of high-quality businesses. In some cases, we bought the whole business. And in some cases, we just bought a big block of stock. But when you analyze what happened, the big money's been made in the high-quality businesses. And most of the other people who've made a lot of money have done so in high-quality businesses.
>
> —CHARLIE MUNGER, USC BUSINESS SCHOOL, 1994

Munger believes the greater the quality of a company, the greater the strength of the wind at your back over the long term.

How do Munger and Buffett assess quality?

> Leaving the question of price aside, the best business to own is one that, over an extended period, can employ large amounts of incremental capital at very high rates of return. The worst business to own is one that must, or will, do the opposite—that is, consistently employ ever-greater amounts of capital at very low rates of return.
>
> —WARREN BUFFETT, 1992 BERKSHIRE SHAREHOLDER LETTER, 1993

Munger and Buffett are very focused on both the magnitude and persistence of the ability of a business to earn a return on capital. Return on invested capital (ROIC) is the ratio of after-tax operating profit divided by the amount of capital invested in the business. In short, how much a business earns on the capital employed in its business determines the quality of that business for Munger and Buffett. Growth of the business is, by itself, neither good nor bad. In the same 1992 letter, Buffett wrote:

> Growth benefits investors only when the business in point can invest at incremental returns that are enticing—in other words, only when each dollar used to finance the growth creates over a dollar of long-term market value.
>
> —WARREN BUFFETT, 1992 BERKSHIRE SHAREHOLDER LETTER, 1993

Eighth Variable: Determining What Businesses to Own (in Whole or in Part)

> We need to have a business with some characteristics that give us a durable competitive advantage.
>
> —CHARLIE MUNGER, BBC INTERVIEW, 2009

> You really have to know a lot about business. You have to know a lot about competitive advantage. You have to know a lot about the maintainability of competitive advantage. You have to have a mind that quantifies things in terms of value. And you have to compare those values with other values available in the stock market.
>
> —CHARLIE MUNGER, *KIPLINGER*, 2005

> Judge the staying quality of the business in terms of its competitive advantage.
>
> —CHARLIE MUNGER, *HARVARD LAW BULLETIN*, 2001

> We buy barriers. Building them is tough. . . . Our great brands aren't anything we've created. We've bought them. If you're buying something at a huge discount to its replacement value and it's hard to replace, you have a big advantage. One competitor is enough to ruin a business running on small margins.
>
> —CHARLIE MUNGER, BERKSHIRE ANNUAL MEETING, 2012

> We're partial to putting out large amounts of money where we won't have to make another decision.
>
> —CHARLIE MUNGER, BERKSHIRE ANNUAL MEETING, 2001

> The difference between a good business and a bad business is that good businesses throw up one easy decision after another. The bad businesses throw up painful decisions time after time.
>
> —CHARLIE MUNGER, BERKSHIRE ANNUAL MEETING, 1997

Why do some businesses create easy decisions for entrepreneurs and investors? A significant part of the answer lies in microeconomics: if there's no significant barrier to entry that creates a *sustainable competitive advantage*, inevitable competition will cause the return on investment for that business to drop to opportunity cost and there will be no economic profit for the producer. The analogy they use at Berkshire is that the business itself should be viewed as the equivalent of a castle and the value of that castle will be determined by the strength of the protective *moat*.

Whether a business has a durable moat is without question the most important attribute for an investor like Munger. He describes a moat in two different ways, each emphasizing the importance of the moat being able to maintain itself over time:

> We have to have a business with some inherent characteristics that give it a durable competitive advantage.
>
> —CHARLIE MUNGER, BBC INTERVIEW, 2009

> We're trying to buy businesses with sustainable competitive advantages at a low—or even a fair price.
>
> —CHARLIE MUNGER, BERKSHIRE ANNUAL MEETING, 2004

A more detailed description of the elements of a moat is set out in the appendix titled Moats. If you have made it this far in this book and have decided to "operationalize" Buffett and Munger's version of the Graham value investing system (which includes considering the quality of the business), you will need to deeply understand the nature of moats. Cigar-butt Graham value investors may argue that they have less need to understand the nature of the moats that companies have, but I believe a sound knowledge of moats is still valuable even for them. As I have written previously in this book, to evaluate the quality of a business, you must understand the fundamentals of business. For some people this will be boring, while others (like me) find it fascinating. If you find this topic boring, the odds that you will be a successful Graham value investor drop substantially.

7
THE RIGHT STUFF IN A BUSINESS

SOME READERS OF this book about Charlie Munger's implementation of the Graham value investing system will probably wonder why it devotes so much time to what one might call the fundamentals of business. If you start thinking this way, please remind yourself that a financial asset, like a share of stock, is not a piece of paper; rather, it is a proportional share in an underlying business. You cannot be a successful Graham value investor if you do not understand the underlying business.

One major fundamental aspect of any business is management. Munger and Buffett are famous for delegating almost all authority and responsibility to Berkshire subsidiaries to run their own business, with the exception of capital allocation and the creation of compensation systems. In other words, while management of the businesses within Berkshire is extremely decentralized, the management of capital allocation and compensation systems is extremely centralized.

1. Capital Allocation Skills

The primary management activity at Berkshire is capital allocation. Munger wrote:

> Proper allocation of capital is an investor's number one job.
>
> —CHARLIE MUNGER, *POOR CHARLIE'S ALMANACK*, 2005

The most important task in capital allocation for Buffett and Munger is to take cash generated by a company like See's Candies and deploy it to the very best opportunity at Berkshire. Buffett's view on the importance of capital allocation is easily stated:

> Charles T. Munger, Berkshire Hathaway's vice-chairman, and I really have only two jobs. . . . One is to attract and keep outstanding managers to run our various operations. The other is capital allocation.
>
> —WARREN BUFFETT, *THE ESSAYS OF WARREN BUFFETT*, 2011

Munger and Buffett believe that capital allocation is a skill that many managers simply do not learn before they become chief executive officers (CEOs) of companies. They believe that a new CEO may have risen from marketing, sales, law, or operations and have little actual capital allocation experience. They believe this can create big problems for a business because the CEO will often not know how to make critical decisions that will maximize shareholder return. It is wise to remember that when someone is selling, they are doing so for a reason. Buffett illustrated this point with an anecdote: A man says to a veterinarian: "Can you help me? Sometimes my horse walks just fine and sometimes he limps."

The vet replied: "Not a problem. When he's walking fine, sell him."[1]

The most important task in capital allocation is to take cash generated by a company and deploy it to the very best opportunity and avoid what Buffett called the *institutional imperative*:

> Rationality frequently wilts when the institutional imperative comes into play. For example: (1) As if governed by Newton's First Law of Motion, an institution will resist any change in its current direction; (2) just as work expands to fill available time, corporate projects or acquisitions will materialize to soak up available funds; (3) any business craving of the leader, however foolish, will be quickly supported by detailed rate-of-return and strategic studies prepared by his troops; and (4) the behavior of peer companies, whether they are expanding, acquiring, setting executive compensation or whatever, will be mindlessly imitated.
>
> —WARREN BUFFETT, BERKSHIRE ANNUAL MEETING, 1989

The culture at Berkshire has been created by Buffett and Munger so as to reject the institutional imperative like a foreign body. Buffett has devoted considerable time to making sure this attribute is part of his legacy to Berkshire. He has written that at Berkshire "a managerial wish list will not be filled at shareholder expense" and continued his lecture:

> Many managerial [princes] remain serenely confident about the future potency of their kisses—even after their corporate backyards are knee-deep in unresponsive toads.
>
> —WARREN BUFFETT, 1981 BERKSHIRE SHAREHOLDER LETTER, 1982

> The heads of many companies are not skilled in capital allocation. Their inadequacy is not surprising. Most bosses rise to the top because they have excelled in an area such as marketing, production, engineering, administration or, sometimes, institutional politics. Once they become CEOs, they face new responsibilities. They now must make capital allocation decisions, a critical job that they may have never tackled and that is not easily mastered.... CEOs who recognize their lack of capital-allocation skills (which not all do) will often try to compensate by turning to their staffs,

management consultants, or investment bankers. Charlie and I have frequently observed the consequences of such "help." On balance, we feel it's more likely to accentuate the capital-allocation problem than to solve it. In the end, plenty of unintelligent capital allocation takes place in corporate America. (That's why you hear so much about "restructuring.")

—WARREN BUFFETT, 1987 BERKSHIRE ANNUAL LETTER, 1988

2. Compensation Systems That Create Alignment with Shareholders

Munger believes that compensation systems are too important to delegate:

It isn't enough to buy the right business. You also have to have a compensation system that's satisfactory to the people running them. At Berkshire Hathaway, we have no [single] system; we have different systems. They're very simple and we don't tend to revisit them very often. It's amazing how well it's worked. We wrote a one-page deal with Chuck Huggins when we bought See's and it's never been touched. We have never hired a compensation consultant.

—CHARLIE MUNGER, WESCO ANNUAL MEETING, 2005

A man does not deserve huge amounts of pay for creating tiny spreads on huge amounts of money. Any idiot can do it. And, as a matter of fact, many idiots do.

—CHARLIE MUNGER, WESCO ANNUAL MEETING, 2009

I'd rather throw a viper down my shirt front than hire a compensation consultant.

—CHARLIE MUNGER, BERKSHIRE ANNUAL MEETING, 2004

This task is particularly hard in the case of Berkshire because the Berkshire managers, in most cases, are already rich and have little financial need to work. For this reason, Munger and Buffett select managers who love what they do enough that financial motivation is only part of the reason to work as CEOs. Someone who knows many of the Berkshire CEOs well once told me that they love working for Buffett and Munger and that the level of personal loyalty to the two billionaires who run Berkshire is quite high. The best place to see the Berkshire compensation philosophy set out is in the Berkshire *Owner's Manual*, which can be found on the Berkshire web site: http://www.berkshirehathaway.com/owners.htm.

Micromanaging what the CEOs of their portfolio companies do is not part of the Berkshire playbook, says Munger.

> In any big business, you don't worry whether someone is doing something wrong, you worry about whether it's big and whether it's material. You can do a lot to mitigate bad behavior, but you simply can't prevent it altogether.
>
> —CHARLIE MUNGER, BERKSHIRE ANNUAL MEETING, 2012

Of course, fear of micromanagement is not a reason to abdicate all management responsibilities. A board of directors letting a parade of managers run down a business is not justified by a fear of micromanagement. Delegation to the extent practiced by Berkshire Hathaway only works if you follow this rule as described by Munger:

> Our success has come from the lack of oversight we've provided, and our success will continue to be from a lack of oversight. But if you're going to provide minimal oversight, you have to buy carefully. It's a different model from GE's. GE's works—it's just very different from ours.
>
> —CHARLIE MUNGER, NOTES FROM THE BERKSHIRE HATHAWAY ANNUAL MEETING, 2005

3. Moat-Widening Skills

Munger would rather have a great moat than great managers. Of course, he would rather have both, so he has a greater margin of safety. To make this point, Buffett commented that, "Good jockeys will do well on good horses, but not on broken down nags."[2] For example, both the New England textile business and the department stores that Berkshire owned in its very early years had competent managers, but the underlying businesses the managers were employed to run were lodged in quicksand. No amount of managerial skill could have fixed the problems at these companies. As another example, Ron Johnson, who formerly was in charge of Apple's retail operations, may be a great manager of a retail business, but the fact that the next business he ran (JC Penney) was fundamentally a lousy business made the critical difference in terms of a financial result.

Munger admits there are rare exceptions in which the quality of the business is less of a driving factor:

> So you do get an occasional opportunity to get into a wonderful business that's being run by a wonderful manager. And, of course, that's hog heaven day. If you don't load up when you get those opportunities, it's a big mistake. . . . Averaged out, betting on the quality of business is better than betting on the quality of management. In other words, if you have to choose one, bet on the business momentum, not the brilliance of the manager. But, very rarely, you find a manager who's so good that you're wise to follow him into what looks like a mediocre business.
>
> —CHARLIE MUNGER, USC BUSINESS SCHOOL, 1994

> The only duty of a corporate executive is to widen the moat. We must make it wider. Every day is to widen the moat. We gave you a competitive advantage, and you must leave us the moat. There are times when it's too tough. But duty should be to widen the moat.

> I can see instance after instance where that isn't what people do in business. One must keep their eye on the ball of widening the moat, to be a steward of the competitive advantage that came to you. A General in England said, "Get you the sons your fathers got, and God will save the Queen." At Hewlett Packard, your responsibility is to train and deliver a subordinate who can succeed you. It's not all that complicated—all that mumbo jumbo. We make bricks in Texas which use the same process as in Mesopotamia.
>
> —CHARLIE MUNGER, WESCO ANNUAL MEETING, 2008

Munger wants managers of the business who have *an ownership mentality* toward the business, not just the attitude of manager.

> Carnegie was always proud that he took very little salary. Rockefeller and Vanderbilt were the same. It was a common culture in a different era. All of these people thought of themselves as the founder. I was delighted to get rid of the pressure of getting fees based on performance. If you're highly conscientious and you hate to disappoint, you will feel the pressure to live up to your incentive fee. There was an enormous advantage [to switching away from taking a percentage of the profits to managing Berkshire, in which their interests as shareholders are exactly aligned with other shareholders].
>
> —CHARLIE MUNGER, BERKSHIRE ANNUAL MEETING, 2003

Munger and Buffett also want managers to have what Nassim Taleb calls "skin in the game."[3] They hate situations in which the result is: heads, managers win and tails, managers do not lose. They want risk and benefits to be symmetrically allocated. For Munger, the presence of the right incentives for a manager is critical. Buffett added that he wants to see managers have "a major portion of their net worth invested in the company. We eat our own cooking."[4]

Munger also fears bureaucracy and Berkshire works hard to prevent it from lowering returns by creating what they call a seamless web of deserved trust.

> For example, if you worked for AT&T in my day, it was a great bureaucracy. Who in the hell was really thinking about the shareholder or anything else? And in a bureaucracy, you think the work is done when it goes out of your in-basket into somebody else's in-basket. But, of course, it isn't. It's not done until AT&T delivers what it's supposed to deliver. So you get big, fat, dumb, unmotivated bureaucracies. . . . The constant curse of scale is that it leads to big, dumb bureaucracy—which, of course, reaches its highest and worst form in government, where the incentives are really awful. That doesn't mean we don't need governments—because we do. But it's a terrible problem to get big bureaucracies to behave.
>
> —CHARLIE MUNGER, UNIVERSITY OF SOUTHERN CALIFORNIA (USC) BUSINESS SCHOOL, 1994

4. Management Already in Place with Integrity

Munger has made it clear that integrity, as a business attribute, is just as important as talent. Most important, Munger values integrity for itself. Working with people who have integrity is its own reward. As a bonus, being able to count on the integrity of a manager is efficient because it means that fewer resources are required to ensure honesty and compliance.

> We would vastly prefer a management in place with a lot of integrity and talent.
>
> —CHARLIE MUNGER, BBC INTERVIEW, 2009

For Munger, a zero-tolerance policy applies to anything related to a lack of integrity. In other words, a standard of "mostly honest" is not a goal for Munger when it comes to integrity. Buffett repeatedly had pointed out that a reputation gained over a lifetime can be lost in less than a second. Munger believes:

> Remember that reputation and integrity are your most valuable assets—and can be lost in a heartbeat.
>
> —CHARLIE MUNGER, *POOR CHARLIE'S ALMANACK*, 2005

Hoping that the negative impact of some dishonest people can be managed by mixing them in with honest people is a triumph of hope over experience in Munger's view.

> When you mix raisins with turds, they are still turds.
>
> —CHARLIE MUNGER, BERKSHIRE ANNUAL MEETING, 2000

It can be harder to spot a lack of integrity than many people imagine, and the consequences can be significant. Munger makes it clear that he has no desire to buy an otherwise "good" business with lousy management and then try to find someone to run it:

> We don't train executives, we find them. If a mountain stands up like Everest, you don't have to be a genius to figure out that it's a high mountain.
>
> —CHARLIE MUNGER, BERKSHIRE ANNUAL MEETING, 2006

Munger and Buffett are not interested in investing in company "turnarounds," because they seldom actually do turn around. Munger wants the moat of the company he is investing in to be strong enough to survive bad management. As was discussed previously, he would prefer to have a moat that is so strong that it could survive if the company was run by "an idiot." Neither Buffett nor Munger is going to buy a business and let some friend or relative run it. However, if they hypothetically did, they would hope that it would still perform adequately as a business with an idiot manager due to the moat.

> Network TV [in its heyday,] anyone could run and do well. If Tom Murphy is running it, you'd do very well, but even your idiot nephew could do well.
>
> —CHARLIE MUNGER, BERKSHIRE HATHAWAY ANNUAL MEETING, 2006

Munger is not saying that management does not matter. Instead, he is saying that he would prefer to have a business that passes the idiot manager test and for the business to have talented management. Owning a business that has lousy underlying economics and that is facing one hard problem after another may not have a good financial outcome even with a top-notch management team, according to Munger. In that sense, having a moat and talented management, such as the team that runs the Berkshire portfolio company Iscar, gives Buffett and Munger an extra margin of safety when making an investment.

5. The Rare Exceptional Manager

Occasionally, Munger and Buffett find a person who has such superior talent that they really do not need much of a moat. This situation is rare, but it does happen.

> Occasionally, you'll find a human being who's so talented that he can do things that ordinary skilled mortals can't. I would argue that Simon Marks—who was second generation in Marks & Spencer of England—was such a man. Patterson was such a man at National Cash Register. And Sam Walton was such a man. These people do come along—and in many cases, they're not all that hard to identity. If they've got a reasonable hand—with the fanaticism and intelligence and so on that these people generally bring to the party—then management can matter much. However, averaged out, betting on the quality of a business is better than betting on the quality of

management. In other words, if you have to choose one, bet on the business momentum, not the brilliance of the manager. But, very rarely, you find a manager who's so good that you're wise to follow him into what looks like a mediocre business.

—CHARLIE MUNGER, USC BUSINESS SCHOOL, 1994

Sometimes, as is the case with Berkshire itself, it is worthwhile to bet on a superior manager. Munger has said:

There are people—very few—worth paying up to get in with for a long-term advantage.

—CHARLIE MUNGER, *DAMN RIGHT*, 2000

Buffett has pointed out that the talents of Ajit Jain in the reinsurance business are just such a case. Buffett said at the most recent Berkshire meeting, "Ajit Jain has created tens of billions of dollars in value for this company out of nothing but brain and hard work." That is high praise indeed, because there's no mention of any moat in that business by Munger and Buffett.

Munger feels that the management of a company like Costco is a case in which management adds to the company moat. For example, he is a huge fan of Costco's James Sinegal. But he clearly feels that companies which have managers like Costco are not easy to find.

I think it's dangerous to rely on special talents—it's better to own lots of monopolistic businesses with unregulated prices. But that's not the world today. We have made money exercising our talents and will continue to do so. I'm glad we have insurance, though it's not a no-brainer, I'm warning you. We have to be smart to make this work.

—CHARLIE MUNGER, WESCO ANNUAL MEETING, 2002

Munger also believes that a skilled manager can sometimes find a relatively safe market niche:

> I find it quite useful to think of a free-market economy—or partly free-market economy—as sort of the equivalent of an ecosystem. Just as animals flourish in niches, people who specialize in some narrow niche can do very well.
>
> —CHARLIE MUNGER, USC BUSINESS SCHOOL, 1994

This strategy is similar to what Professor Michael Porter calls "differentiation."[5] This approach can be workable, but it is inherently riskier to try to find a haven from competition in a niche than to have a moat (sometimes it is better to have both). An example of a niche market in which Munger and Buffett believe they found a gem of a management team is Iscar:

> Judging the management at a company like Iscar is easy—those people are enormously talented and wonderful. But there aren't many managements like that and few people with the incentive of such intensity.
>
> —CHARLIE MUNGER, WESCO ANNUAL MEETING, 2011

> The reason I got so high on it so fast was that the people are so outstandingly talented. The idea of being in business with them just struck me worth straining for. We didn't know when we were young which things to stretch for, but by the time we reached Iscar, which we never would have bought when we were young, we knew to stretch for the right people. It's a hell of a business. Everything is right there. Isn't it good that we keep learning? Better late than never.
>
> —CHARLIE MUNGER, WESCO ANNUAL MEETING, 2007

This description by Bill Gates of the Berkshire philosophy on the importance of management to a business is a very useful summary:

> [Warren's] penchant for long-term investments is reflected in another aphorism: 'You should invest in a business that even a fool can run, because someday a fool will.' He doesn't believe in businesses that

> rely for their success on every employee being excellent. Nor does he believe that great people help all that much when the fundamentals of a business are bad. He says that when good management is brought into a fundamentally bad business, it's the reputation of the business that remains intact. Warren installs strong managers in the companies Berkshire owns, and tends to leave them pretty much alone. His basic proposition to managers is that to the degree that a company spins off cash, which good businesses do, the managers can trust Warren to invest it wisely. He doesn't encourage managers to diversify. Managers are expected to concentrate on the businesses they know well so that Warren is free to concentrate on what he does well: invest.
>
> —BILL GATES, *FORTUNE*, 1996

With that last bit of wisdom, I send you off into to the world, hoping that you too learn to concentrate and invest successfully. Whenever in doubt about making a decision related to investing (or otherwise), ask yourself this: *What would Charlie Munger do?*

BERKSHIRE MATH

IN MAKING AN *intrinsic value* calculation, Berkshire uses the long-term (30-year) U.S. Treasury rate as the discount rate. This is not a typical approach, and many people do not fully understand why Berkshire uses this rate. Buffett explained:

> We use the risk-free rate merely to equate one item to another. In other words, we're looking for whatever is the most attractive. In order to estimate the present value of anything, we're going to use a number. And, obviously, we can always buy government bonds. Therefore, that becomes the yardstick rate . . . to simply compare all kinds of investment opportunities across the spectrum.
>
> —WARREN BUFFET, BERKSHIRE ANNUAL MEETING, 1997

What is happening in this process is an examination of opportunity cost.

> Intelligent people make decisions based on opportunity costs—in other words, it's your alternatives that matter. That's how we make all of our decisions.
>
> —CHARLIE MUNGER, BERKSHIRE ANNUAL MEETING, 2003

Munger thinks about the opportunity cost of capital by considering what the alternatives are for that capital. Buffett has said, "Charlie and I don't know our cost of capital. . . . We measure everything against our alternatives."[1] Why would you buy an investment that is not in your top 2 percent of opportunities? As has been explained previously, this will lead to a concentrated portfolio that is perfectly acceptable to Munger. Because he believes that risk comes from not knowing what you are doing, he has adopted a focused investing style, which will be explained below.

"How does Munger account for risk when he buys an asset?" He will only invest if he strongly believes the current earnings are *nearly certain* to continue. While most other investors will adjust the discount rate for what they may believe to be greater risk, Berkshire wants essentially no risk as a starting point. In other words, rather than adjust the discount rate to account for risk, Munger and Buffett use a risk-free rate to compare alternative investments. They look for both conservatively determined fundamentals and a stable business history, which indicate to them that the current state of the business in question will continue. However, to provide a cushion against mistakes, they will not actually buy an asset without at least a 25 percent discount in intrinsic value (this discount is their margin of safety).

The theory behind Munger's very different approach to dealing with risk is worth examining in detail. As a review, risk is the possibility of suffering a loss (not price volatility). The way Berkshire deals with risk is by buying what they feel is a conservatively valued asset with no risk at a discount price. Their focus is on having protection against mistakes that they may make during that process. What they do not do is increase the interest rate used in the computation to deal with risks inherent in the business. If there are significant risks inherent in the business itself, they put the decision in the *too hard* pile and move on to other potential opportunities.

The mathematical process that Munger and Buffett use at Berkshire is simple. (Please do not stop reading because I used the word *mathematics.*) First, Berkshire calculates the past and current "owner's earnings" of the business. Then they insert into the formula a reasonable and conservative growth rate of the owner's earnings. They solve for the present value of the owner's earnings by discounting using the 30-year U.S. Treasury rate. The focus of the investing process at Berkshire is on return on equity (ROE), not earnings per share (EPS). As an aside, Munger believes that every manager of a business should be thinking about intrinsic value when making all capital allocation decisions. Note that Berkshire does not use price to earnings multiples in calculating value. Owner's earnings is a very specific type of earnings, and they stick to that set of figures.

In determining *intrinsic value*, Munger doesn't swallow the stories of promoters who sing songs and tell tall tales about EBITDA (earnings before interest, taxes, depreciation, and amortization) and non-GAAP (generally accepted accounting principles) "earnings." He likes genuine free cash flow. He considers "drowning in cash" to be a very good thing indeed. On the topic of non-GAPP earnings, Munger has said this:

> I don't even like to hear the word EBITDA.
>
> —CHARLIE MUNGER, Q&A WITH SIX BUSINESS SCHOOLS, 2009

MOATS

MUNGER HAS NOT explained his theories on what creates and sustains a moat as comprehensively as Buffett, but he has made some comments that point people in the right direction.

The five primary elements that can help create a moat are as follows:

1. *Supply-Side Economies of Scale and Scope*

If a company's average costs fall when more of a product or service is produced, there are supply-side *economies of scale*. Intel is a classic example of a business that benefits from economies of scale. In Munger's view, Wal-Mart has substantial supply-side economies of scale through its investments in distribution and other systems. Companies that operate huge steel plants and shipyards can also have supply-side economies of scale. Munger described two different supply-side economies of scale:

> On the subject of economies of scale, I find chain stores quite interesting. Just think about it. The concept of a chain store was a

fascinating invention. You get this huge purchasing power—which means that you have lower merchandise costs. You get a whole bunch of little laboratories out there in which you can conduct experiments. And you get specialization. If one little guy is trying to buy across twenty-seven different merchandise categories influenced by traveling salesmen, he's going to make a lot of dumb decisions. But if your buying is done in headquarters for a huge bunch of stores, you can get very bright people who know a lot about refrigerators and so forth to do the buying. The reverse is demonstrated by the little store where one guy is doing all the buying. So there are huge purchasing advantages.

Some [supply-side advantages] come from simple geometry. If you're building a great circular tank, obviously as you build it bigger, the amount of steel you use in the surface goes up with the square and the cubic volume goes up with the cube. So as you increase the dimensions, you can hold a lot more volume per unit area of steel. There are all kinds of things like that where the simple geometry—the simple reality—gives you an advantage of scale.

—CHARLIE MUNGER, UNIVERSITY OF SOUTHERN CALIFORNIA (USC) BUSINESS SCHOOL, 1994

You can get advantages of scale from TV advertising. When TV advertising first arrived—when talking color pictures first came into our living rooms—it was an unbelievably powerful thing. And in the early days, we had three networks that had whatever it was—say 90 percent of the audience. Well, if you were Procter & Gamble, you could afford to use this new method of advertising. You could afford the very expensive cost of network television because you were selling so damn many cans and bottles. Some little guy couldn't. And there was no way of buying it in part. Therefore, he couldn't use it. In effect, if you didn't have a big volume, you couldn't use network TV advertising—which was the most effective technique. So when

> TV came in, the branded companies that were already big got a huge tail wind.
>
> —CHARLIE MUNGER, USC BUSINESS SCHOOL, 1994

Although Berkshire was a bit late to appreciate the financial attractiveness of the railroad business, Munger and Buffett clearly value the moat that supply-side economies of scale create in that business. A new competitor in the railroad business is highly unlikely. If the public roads deteriorate because the United States underinvests in infrastructure, Buffett and Munger believe railroads will become even more valuable. Munger is very positive on the future of the railroad business.

> Do you know what it would cost to replace Burlington Northern today? We are not going to build another transcontinental. And those assets are valuable, have utility. Now they want to raise diesel prices on trucks. . . . We finally realized that railroads now have a huge competitive advantage, with double stacked rail cars, guided by computers, moving more and more production from China, etc. They have a big advantage over truckers in huge classes of business.
>
> —CHARLIE MUNGER, WESCO ANNUAL MEETING, 2008

> We don't know how to buy stocks by metrics. . . . We know that Burlington Northern will have a competitive advantage in years. . . . We don't know what the heck Apple will have. . . . You really have to understand the company and its competitive positions. . . . That's not disclosed by the math.
>
> —CHARLIE MUNGER, BERKSHIRE ANNUAL MEETING, 2013

The railroad industry is interesting in that long ago they were a growth industry that created both great fortunes and great busts in the aftermath of that success. There were many times in history when railroads were very lousy investments.

Regarding the impact of supply-side economies of scale, Munger has pointed out:

> In some businesses, the very nature of things cascades toward the overwhelming dominance of one firm. It tends to cascade to a winner-take-all result. And these advantages of scale are so great, for example, that when Jack Welch came into General Electric, he just said, "to hell with it. We're either going to be number one or two in every field we're in or we're going to be out." That was a very tough-minded thing to do, but I think it was a correct decision if you're thinking about maximizing shareholder wealth.
>
> —CHARLIE MUNGER, USC BUSINESS SCHOOL, 1994

If it is cost efficient for a company to produce several different products or services, a company can also benefit from supply-side *economies of scope.* To benefit from economies of scope, a business must share resources across markets while keeping the amount of those resources largely fixed. Businesses that desire to benefit from economies of scope must avoid running as isolated units.

2. *Demand-Side Economies of Scale (Network Effects)*

Demand-side economies of scale (also known as "network effects") result when a product or service becomes more valuable as more people use it. Craigslist, eBay, Twitter, Facebook, and other so-called *multi-sided markets* have demand-side economies of scale that operate on their behalf. American Express is an example of a company in the Berkshire portfolio with network effect benefits; the more merchants that accept their card, the more valuable the service gets, and the more people who use the card, the more valuable the services are for merchants. Munger has said:

> It would be easier to screw up American Express than Coke or Gillette, but it's an immensely strong business.
>
> —CHARLIE MUNGER, BERKSHIRE ANNUAL MEETING, 2000

A company having beneficial network effects is only one dimension that impacts profit. Sometimes, network effects exist but the market is small because it is a niche. Amazon's market is massive, and that matters greatly in terms of the market capitalization it can generate. Some network effects are very strong and some are weak.

Some companies have both demand-side and supply-side economies of scale. Amazon has both supply-side and demand-side economies of scale, and they reinforce each other. The more people who provide comments on Amazon, the more valuable it becomes to other users due to demand-side economies. Amazon also has huge advantages with their warehouses and the supply chain on the supply side.

3. *Brand*

Understanding how Munger thinks about brand is best illustrated by an example. For many years, Munger was the chairman of a company called Wesco Financial. At the 2011 meeting of Wesco, which was held just before it was merged into Berkshire Hathaway, Munger admitted that he and Buffett really did not understand the value of a brand until they bought See's Candies.

See's Candies is also a great side-by-side test of brand power. To illustrate, if you grew up in a home that bought See's Candies (mostly on the West Coast, especially in California,) and your experiences around that candy have very favorable associations, you will pay more for a box bearing the See's Candies brand. By contrast, someone who grew up on the East Coast of the United States will not attribute much value to that brand because they do not have those same experiences. For this reason, See's Candies has found it hard to expand regionally and has done so very slowly. What See's Candies sells is not just food, but rather an experience. Because box candy sales are highest during holiday seasons, the financial results of the company are also very lumpy. See's Candies generates losses two quarters a year and makes all its profit in the other two quarters around three holidays.

Buffett talks about the fact that building some brands took many decades:

> When you were a 16-year-old, you took a box of candy on your first date with a girl and gave it either to her parents or to her. In California the girls slap you when you bring Russell Stover, and kiss you when you bring See's. . . . I don't think See's means anything to people on the East Coast, where people are also exposed to higher-end chocolate products.
>
> —WARREN BUFFET, "THE SECRETS OF SEE'S CANDIES," *FORTUNE MAGAZINE*, 2012

While some of the power of a brand can come from taste, modern flavor firms can replicate almost any taste. Trade dress and presentation of a good or service matters more than ever. A lot of Tiffany's brand power lies in the blue box the jewelry comes in. Coke made a massive mistake thinking it was flavor that mattered most in a blind taste test when it introduced New Coke. When the taste test was not blind, Coke won; when it was blind, Coke did not win. Munger said once about the New Coke episode:

> [Coke spent] 100 years getting people to believe that trademark had all these intangible values too. And people associate it with a flavor. . . . Pepsi was within weeks of coming out with old Coke in a Pepsi bottle, which would've been the biggest fiasco in modern times. Perfect insanity.
>
> —CHARLIE MUNGER, HARVARD UNIVERSITY, 1995

A moat powered by a brand is something very different from one created via supply-side or demand-side economies of scale. For example, Buffett believes that for a company like Disney, when the brand is mentioned in conversation "you have something in your mind." He added:

> How would you try to create a brand that competes with Disney? Coke is a brand associated with people being happy around the world. That is what you want to have in a business. That is the moat. You want that moat to widen.
>
> —WARREN BUFFETT, VANDERBILT VISIT NOTES, 2005

Brands, of course, can fail over time. Put a luxury brand on a shelf at Costco, as some have done, and that luxury brand can be damaged for certain customers. License it too broadly and the brand can also be damaged. Buffett and Munger are attracted to brands that they use in their own lives. See's Candies and Dairy Queen are just two examples.

Some brands incur problems with their brand that are completely self-inflicted. Buffett went on to say about one of his most favorite brands:

> Take See's Candies. You cannot destroy the brand of See's Candies. Only See's can do that. You have to look at the brand as a promise to the customer that we are going to offer the quality and service that is expected. We link the product with happiness. You don't see See's Candies sponsoring the local funeral home. We are at the Thanksgiving Day parades though.
>
> —WARREN BUFFETT, NOTES FROM UNIVERSITY OF GEORGIA VISIT, 2007

Regarding brand power, the two Berkshire leaders have often cited Wrigley's as a brand that creates a strong moat. Munger has pointed out:

> The informational advantage of brands is hard to beat. And your advantage of scale can be an informational advantage. If I go to some remote place, I may see Wrigley chewing gum alongside Glotz's chewing gum. Well, I know that Wrigley is a satisfactory product, whereas I don't know anything about Glotz's. So if one is $0.40 and the other is $0.30, am I going to take something I don't

> know and put it in my mouth—which is a pretty personal place, after all—for a lousy dime? So, in effect, Wrigley, simply by being so well known, has advantages of scale—what you might call an informational advantage. Everyone is influenced by what others do and approve. Another advantage of scale comes from psychology. The psychologists use the term "social proof." We are all influenced—subconsciously and to some extent consciously—by what we see others do and approve. Therefore, if everybody's buying something, we think it's better. We don't like to be the one guy who's out of step. Again, some of this is at a subconscious level and some of it isn't. Sometimes, we consciously and rationally think, "Gee, I don't know much about this. They know more than I do. Therefore, why shouldn't I follow them?" All told, your advantages can add up to one tough moat.
>
> —CHARLIE MUNGER, USC BUSINESS SCHOOL, 1994

A very important test for Buffett and Munger in determining the strength of a brand-based moat is whether a competitor can replicate or weaken the moat with a massive checkbook. As just one example, here is what Buffett said about Coke at the 2012 Berkshire meeting: "If you gave me $10, $20, $30 billion to knock off Coca-Cola, I couldn't do it."[1] That is in his view what defines a strong moat. Firms like Nike and BMW each have brands that help maintain their moat, which were hard to get and are super valuable to have. Michael Mauboussin wrote: "Brands do not confer advantages in and of themselves. Brands only increase value if they increase customer willingness to pay or reduce the cost to provide the good or service."[2] The creation of a great brand is a rare thing that requires considerable skill—and arguably a big dose of luck as well.

4. *Regulation*

Certain businesses have created a competence with regard to regulation that is so strong that the regulation itself actually serves as a moat. Regulations can often end up protecting existing entrenched producers rather than helping consumers. For example, some people believe banks have created such a powerful layer of regulatory expertise that the regulators have become captured by the industry they regulate. Similarly, there are a number of professional guilds, like lawyers, that have been able to use regulation to limit supply.

For Berkshire, the regulation-driven moat that Moody's possessed in the bond rating business was a big attraction. To issue bonds, regulators actually require that the issuer get an opinion from a very small number of bond rating firms, which means that rating firms like Moody's, S&P, and Fitch have a moat. When regulation disappears, it often becomes quickly evident that it was a major factor in industry profitability. In other words, you find out who is swimming naked when the regulatory-driven moat disappears.

5. Patents and Intellectual Property

Companies that have been granted a patent, trademark, or other type of intellectual property by the government have in effect been given a legal monopoly. This barrier to entry can create a substantial moat for the owner of the intellectual property. You may or may not think too many patents have been granted or have been granted in inappropriate ways, but the value of a patent, once granted, is a different point.

Regarding the value of intellectual property, Munger has said this:

> In microeconomics, of course, you've got the concept of patents, trademarks, exclusive franchises, and so forth. Patents are quite interesting. When I was young, I think more money went into patents than came out. Judges tended to throw them out—based on arguments about what was really invented and what relied on prior art. That isn't altogether clear. But they changed that. They didn't change the laws. They just changed the administration, so that it all goes to one patent court. And that court is now very much more pro-patent. So I think people are now starting to make a lot of

> money out of owning patents. But trademarks and franchises have always been great. Trademarks, of course, have always made people a lot of money. A trademark system is a wonderful thing for a big operation if it's well known.
>
> —CHARLIE MUNGER, USC BUSINESS SCHOOL, 1994

One example of a company that Berkshire values higher due to intellectual property patents is Lubrizol. Buffett said once:

> It struck me as a business I didn't know anything about initially. You know, you're talking about petroleum additives. . . . Are there competitive moats, is there ease of entry, all that sort of thing? I did not have any understanding of that at all initially. And I talked to Charlie a few days later. . . . and Charlie says, "I don't understand it either."
>
> —WARREN BUFFETT, BERKSHIRE ANNUAL MEETING, 2008

Eventually, Buffett was won over and made the Lubrizol purchase. Buffet said once:

> I decided there's probably a good size moat on this. They've got lots and lots of patents, but more than that they have a connection with customers.
>
> —WARREN BUFFETT, BERKSHIRE ANNUAL MEETING, 2008

At the 2011 Berkshire meeting, Buffett reiterated that he decided to go ahead because he thought that the more than 1,600 patents held by Lubrizol would give the company "a durable competitive advantage."

Another example of intellectual property proving its value for Munger occurred in the 1970s, when Russell Stover Candies started to open stores in markets served by See's Candies. The Russell Stover stores were designed to be very similar in appearance to See's Candies stores. By asserting intellectual property rights, Munger was able to get an agreement from Russell Stover to stop opening similar stores through the threat of litigation.

Cumulative Impact of Many Factors

Some businesses, like Berkshire, have been able to create a moat as a result of a combination of better systems and culture than their competitors. One way to understand this point is to look at Berkshire and ask whether it has a moat. In other words, while Berkshire has Buffett and Munger, what else does the company have that acts as a barrier to entry creating sustainable competitive advantage? Berkshire has many elements that make up the whole of its moat, and they are further amplified by the way the elements "fit" together. In short, the aggregate value that these elements create is greater than the sum of the parts.

This section presents a few of the elements that collectively create Berkshire's moat.

1. Berkshire Is Tax Efficient

When a given Berkshire portfolio company (e.g., See's Candies) generates cash, that cash is rarely invested in more See's Candies stores, manufacturing plants, or acquisitions because the return on capital would be lower than other alternatives within Berkshire. Because of Berkshire's structure, Buffett is able to move that cash from See's Candies to the greatest opportunity on a tax-efficient basis (without paying the tax that would be imposed if See's Candies paid a dividend or See's shares were sold and the money reinvested). Buffett elaborated:

> Because we still have this ability to redistribute money in a tax-efficient way within the company, we can reallocate it to where it will earn a higher return than shareholders may on their own.
>
> —WARREN BUFFETT, BERKSHIRE ANNUAL MEETING, 2008

Munger added this:

> Another very simple effect I seldom see discussed by either investment managers or anybody else is the effect of taxes. If you're going to buy something which compounds for 30 years at 15 percent per annum and you pay one 35 percent tax at the very end, the way that works out is that after taxes, you keep 13.3 percent per annum. In contrast, if you bought the same investment but had to pay taxes every year of 35 percent out of the 15 percent that you earned, then your return would be 15 percent minus 35 percent of 15 percent or only 9.75 percent per year compounded. So the difference there is over 3.5 percent. And what 3.5 percent does to the numbers over long holding periods like 30 years is truly eye-opening. If you sit back for long, long stretches in great companies, you can get a huge edge from nothing but the way that income taxes work.
>
> —CHARLIE MUNGER, USC BUSINESS SCHOOL, 1994

> WB talks about increasing book value after paying full corporate taxes of 35 percent. Indices don't have to pay taxes.
>
> —CHARLIE MUNGER, BERKSHIRE ANNUAL MEETING, 2014

2. *Berkshire Has Low Overhead*

At a Wesco meeting, Munger said:

> A lot of people think if you just had more process and more compliance—checks and double-checks and so forth—you could create a better result in the world. Well, Berkshire has had practically no process. We had hardly any internal auditing until they forced it on us. We just try to operate in a seamless web of deserved trust and be careful whom we trust.
>
> —CHARLIE MUNGER, WESCO ANNUAL MEETING, 2007

Trust-based systems in which managers must "eat their own cooking" are core to Berkshire's culture, which translates to lower overhead. The *New York Times* put it this way:

> [Berkshire] has a corporate headquarters with a mere twenty-five people on a single floor of an office building. From there Mr. Buffett and his staff allocate capital and contemplate acquisitions or sales, hire or fire people to run those portfolio companies, and otherwise stay out of the way.
>
> —*NEW YORK TIMES*, 2014

Morningstar added: "All of the firm's operating companies are managed on a decentralized basis, eliminating the need for layers of management control and pushing responsibility down to the subsidiary level, where managers are empowered to make their own decisions."[3]

In order for this "seamless web of deserved trust" system to work, you must have great managers and have the right incentives in place. Berkshire's culture is designed to ensure that anyone who succeeds Buffett will know how to do this. Buffett said at the 2014 Berkshire shareholder's meeting that if Berkshire has a weakness, it is that they tend to over-trust, but with that comes low overhead. The "seamless web of trust" system is itself part of the Berkshire moat.

3. Berkshire Is the Private Buyer of First Resort

If you have spent your life building a business and decide to sell the company, Buffett and Munger offer you a unique opportunity. They will let you (and in fact want you) to continue running the business. Your other option is selling the business to a private equity firm that does not give a damn about your business and will probably load it up with debt, creating a serious risk that the company will fail. Buffett has a track record of keeping the business, instead of playing what Munger calls "a game of gin rummy" with it and other holdings, which makes Berkshire attractive to many sellers of a business.[4]

People who sell businesses to Berkshire are rich enough that they have more money than they will ever need. Berkshire gives the selling owner the chance to make sure that the business they care about and the people that work there continue to thrive. For this reason, Berkshire gets offered the opportunity to buy businesses at very attractive prices. Buffett said in the most recent shareholder's meeting: "Private equity firms buy businesses, but they're looking to sell those holdings down the road."[5] To reassure selling owners, Buffett holds on to businesses even if returns are less than stellar. Here's Buffett on this point:

> You would not get a passing grade in business school if you put down our principles for why we keep some businesses, but we made a promise. If we don't keep our promise, word would get around. We list the economic principles, so managers who sell to us know they can count on it. We can't make some promises, and we don't promise never to sell. But we've only had to get rid of a few businesses, including the original textile business. We also let managers continue to run their business. We are now in a class that is hard to compete with. A private equity firm won't be impressed by what we put in the back of our annual report. People who are rich and run a company their grandfather started—they don't want to hand it over to a couple of MBAs who want to show their stuff. As long as we behave properly, we will maintain that asset, and many will have trouble competing with it.
>
> —WARREN BUFFETT, BERKSHIRE ANNUAL MEETING, 2014

This phenomenon creates a positive reputation for Berkshire and contributes to the moat.

4. *Berkshire Has Permanent Capital*

Berkshire has permanent capital, which greatly enables the company to outperform other investors. Noted Graham value investor Bruce Berkowitz explained:

> That is the secret sauce: permanent capital. That is essential. I think that's the reason Buffett gave up his partnership. You need it, because when push comes to shove, people run. . . . That's why we keep a lot of cash around. . . . Cash is the equivalent of financial Valium. It keeps you cool, calm and collected.
>
> —BRUCE BERKOWITZ, UNIVERSITY OF MIAMI INTERVIEW, 2012

5. Berkshire Outperforms in Down Markets

Because Buffett and Munger are Graham value investors, Berkshire uses an investing approach designed to outperform in "up" markets and overperform in "down" markets. The goal of a value investor is superior absolute performance, not relative performance. Buffett put it simply: "We will underperform in strong years, we will match in medium years, and we will do better in down years. We will outperform over a cycle, but there's no guarantee on that."[6] Other investors, like Seth Klarman, use the same approach. The facts support this conclusion. Ben Carlson pointed out: "It's the down years where Buffett has really extended his lead, outperforming the market by almost 25 percent per year when stocks fall. This is his secret sauce."[7] Howard Marks pointed out the following rules for a value investor: "Rule No. 1: Most things will prove to be cyclical. Rule No. 2: Some of the greatest opportunities for gain and loss come when other people forget Rule No. 1."[8] Buffett has his own version of this which states: "Rule No. 1 is never lose money. Rule No. 2 is never forget rule number one."[9] Berkshire's results must be compared with alternatives on a risk-adjusted basis.

6. Berkshire Benefits from Float

Berkshire's insurance operations generate low-cost float (cash that comes in from insurance premiums collected well in advance of future insurance claims). This float is a major source of funding for investments. At Berkshire, float has grown from $39 million in 1970 to just over $77 billion in 2014, and significant amounts of that cash can be put to work within Berkshire. Because Berkshire has access to float, its financial returns will not be your financial returns unless you also own an insurance company. You will never be as rich as Buffett without access to float. However, that does not mean that you should not be a Graham value investor anyway.

7. High-Quality Shareholders, Including Buffett and Munger

High-quality shareholders don't panic and think long term about investing results. That a company may have a moat at a given time is insufficient. In Munger's view, even if you currently have a very profitable business, that does not mean that profitability will persist for very long. The process of what Joseph Schumpeter called "creative destruction"[10] is as powerful as anything in business. Having a moat is the only way to fight against the tide of competitive destruction.

Michael Mauboussin, in what is arguably the best essay ever on moats, wrote:

> Companies generating high economic returns will attract competitors willing to take a lesser, albeit still attractive, return which will drive down aggregate industry returns to the opportunity cost of capital.
>
> —MICHAEL MAUBOUSSIN, "MEASURING THE MOAT," 2002

For example, if you open a very successful clothing store with certain innovative attributes, that success will attract imitators and competitors. Through a process of creative destruction, some clothing stores will adapt and survive and thrive and others will fail. The consumer wins because the products and services offered to them get better and better. However, this is a painful process for an investor since the outcome can be highly uncertain. It is also the hardest part for a businessperson because failure is an essential part of capitalism.

Given the inevitability of relentless competition, the question to ask, according to Munger, is as follows:

> How do you compete against a true fanatic? You can only try to build the best possible moat and continuously attempt to widen it.
>
> —CHARLIE MUNGER, *POOR CHARLIE'S ALMANACK*, 2005

Jim Sinegal of Costco is just such a fanatic; that's why Munger serves on their board. The founder of Nebraska Furniture Mart, Rose Blumkin ("Mrs. B"), would be another fanatic. Munger loves the management team at Berkshire portfolio company Iscar. Going down the list of Berkshire CEOs reveals a long list of fanatics.

One reason that capitalism works is because moats are hard to create and usually deteriorate over time. What happens over time is that so-called *producer surplus* is transferred into *consumer surplus*. Munger described the competitive process and why it benefits consumers as follows:

> The major success of capitalism is its ability to drench business owners in feedback and allocate talent efficiently. If you have an area with twenty restaurants, and suddenly eighteen are out of business, the remaining two are in good, capable hands. Business owners are constantly being reminded of benefits and punishments. That's psychology explaining economics.
>
> —CHARLIE MUNGER, WESCO ANNUAL MEETING, 2011

Munger's views on the nature of business competition are Darwinian. He believes that capitalism does not pull its punches in markets that are genuinely competitive:

> Over the very long term, history shows that the chances of any business surviving in a manner agreeable to a company's owners are slim at best.
>
> —CHARLIE MUNGER, *THE DHANDHO INVESTOR*, 2007

Capitalism is a pretty brutal place.

—CHARLIE MUNGER, USC BUSINESS SCHOOL, 1994

When it comes to moats, durability matters. Munger wants to avoid a business that has a moat today but loses it tomorrow. Some moats atrophy gradually over time and some fade much more quickly. As Ernest Hemingway said in *The Sun Also Rises*, a business can go bankrupt in two ways: "gradually and then suddenly." The speed of moat destruction has accelerated over time due to advances in technology and the way it spreads information. For some people, this increase in speed can at times be disorienting. For example, the speed with which companies like Kodak or Nortel lost their moats has been shocking to many investors who grew up mostly in another era.

The speed with which a moat disappears should not be confused with cases where a company never had a moat. How long your moat lasts is called your *competitive advantage period* (CAP), according to Michael Mauboussin. The speed of moat dissipation will be different in each case and need not be constant. The rate at which a moat atrophies is similar to what academics call *fade*, argued Michael Mauboussin.[11]

Even the very best companies can see competition make their moats shrink or even disappear. Munger has said:

> Frequently, you'll look at a business having fabulous results. And the question is, "How long can this continue?" Well, there's only one way I know to answer that. And that's to think about why the results are occurring now—and then to figure out what could cause those results to stop occurring.
>
> —CHARLIE MUNGER, *DAMN RIGHT*, 2000

Newspapers are a good example of an industry that once had a fantastic moat but now is in decline. Unfortunately for newspapers, changes in technology have been taking down their moat in rather dramatic fashion.

> The perfectly fabulous economics of this [newspaper] business could become grievously impaired.
>
> —CHARLIE MUNGER, WESCO ANNUAL MEETING, 2000

Munger saw this deterioration before many other people did, most likely because Berkshire owned newspaper properties like the *Washington Post* and *The Buffalo News*. Berkshire has not given up on all types of newspapers. Papers that cover local news, particularly in a city with a strong sense of community, are still attractive for Berkshire. They said at the 2012 Berkshire meeting that they may buy more newspapers. These small-city newspaper purchases seem like a Ben Graham cigar-butt style investment, and for that reason a reversion to an old investing style. But Berkshire has a huge amount of cash to put to work and only so many quality businesses to buy. Munger added:

> Excess cash is an advantage, not a disadvantage.
>
> —CHARLIE MUNGER, BERKSHIRE ANNUAL MEETING, 2012

As a pool of investment dollars gets bigger, it gets harder to find companies to buy or invest in that have a moat. In this sense, size works against investment performance. More than one fund manager has suffered from this problem because the tendency is to ignore the need for a strong moat so you can get large amounts of money put to work.

Kodak is a company that once had a strong moat but then began to lose it drastically. Munger described the competitive destruction that hit the photography business:

> What happened to Kodak is a natural outcome of competitive capitalism.
>
> —CHARLIE MUNGER, CNBC INTERVIEW, 2012

It is true that what happened to Kodak was rough, but the full story according to Munger should take into account that there was a part of Kodak that did have a moat and will survive:

> People think the whole thing failed, but they forget that Kodak didn't really go broke, because Eastman Chemical did survive as a prosperous company and they spun that off.
>
> —CHARLIE MUNGER, *FORTUNE*, 2012

The challenge any company that has lost its moat faces is both substantial and terrifying. Once a feedback loop turns negative, it is hard for any company to regain what it once had. Precisely the factors that created the moat in the first place can tear the company down just as fast or faster. If the ride up was nonlinear, it is very possible that the ride down will be nonlinear as well.

As another example, Munger has said that department stores in downtown areas once had a very strong moat, given the economies of scale and their central locations near mass transit. However, the way people lived started to change as cars became more affordable and people migrated to suburbs with shopping centers. The arrival of Amazon.com in the retail business has further damaged the moat of the big-box retailers of all kinds, whether in the city or the suburbs.

What determines whether a company has a moat is qualitative (e.g., supply-side and demand-side economies of scale, brand, regulation, and intellectual property), but how you test to determine the strength of the moat is quantitative (i.e., it's a mathematical exercise). Mathematical formulas will not tell you how to get a moat, but they can help prove that you have one—at least for now. To test whether you have a moat with a given company, determine if you are earning profits that are greater than your *opportunity cost of capital* (OCC). If that level of profitability has been maintained for some reasonable period (measured in years), then you have a strong moat. If the size of the positive difference between *return on invested capital* (ROIC) and OCC is large and if that spread is persistent over time, your moat is relatively strong. Exactly how long the moat must persist to meet this test is an interesting question. If it is not a period of at least two years, you are taking a significant risk. Five years of supporting data give you more certainty that your moat is sustainable. For more on this subject, read Michael Mauboussin's essay "Measuring the Moat," which is a classic.

Spotting the existence of a moat that has not been fully taken advantage of by its current ownership can be profitable for an investor buying that business. Munger pointed out:

> There are actually businesses that you will find a few times in a lifetime, where any manager could raise the return enormously just by raising prices—and yet they haven't done it. So they have huge untapped pricing power that they're not using. That is the ultimate no-brainer. . . . Disney found that it could raise those prices a lot and the attendance stayed right up. So a lot of the great record of Eisner and Wells . . . came from just raising prices at Disneyland and Disneyworld and through video cassette sales of classic animated movies. . . . At Berkshire Hathaway, Warren and I raised the prices of See's candy a little faster than others might have. And, of course, we invested in Coca-Cola—which had some untapped pricing power. And it also had brilliant management. So a Goizueta and Keough could do much more than raise prices. It was perfect.
>
> —CHARLIE MUNGER, CALIFORNIA INSTITUTE OF TECHNOLOGY, 1997

Starting with See's Candies, Munger and Buffett learned that when you have a great moat (in this case driven by a powerful but primarily regional brand), the business can raise prices to improve profitability. They also learned that some brands translate less well to new markets, and there is a limit on how many box candy stores one can profitably build in a given geographic area.

At a very practical level, the discussion above illustrates that there are some rules of thumb one can use to test the strength of a moat. At the top of the list is whether the business has pricing power. For example, if you must hold a prayer meeting before you try to raise prices, then you do not have much of a moat, if any, argues Buffett.

There's nothing sinister about the term *moat*. Business is, by its very nature, a competitive process. Even a small restaurant selling barbecue can have a moat. A company that has a return on capital significantly greater than its opportunity cost over time has a moat, whether they know it or not.

Munger and Buffett have said that there are also three different skills that relate to moats: creating a moat, identifying a moat that others have created, and identifying a startup that may acquire a moat before it is evident.

Creating a moat is something that people like Ray Kroc, Sam Walton, Estee Lauder, Mary Kay Ash, and Bill Gates have accomplished. Moat creation requires superior management skills, always combined with some degree of luck. It is theoretically possible to acquire a moat with no management talent and just luck, but I can't think of an example of this ever happening. Sometimes people who are fantastic managers and have the ability to create a moat have very poor skills when it comes to investing. Stock promoters love these people because they are big targets for scams.

Identifying a moat others have created is something that people like Munger and Buffett can do. Munger admits that he and Buffett buy moats rather than build them, because building them is not something they do particularly well. In addition to a moat, Munger insists that there be a talented management team already in place. For investors who buy moats instead of creating one, the existence of a moat has special value because they can sometimes survive financially, even if management talent does not deliver as expected or if they leave the business.

Identifying a startup that may acquire a moat before it becomes evident is something that some venture capitalists can do when there is a sufficiently high level of probability that they can generate an attractive return on capital overall. Venture capitalists harvest something called *optionality*, which is a different form of arbitrage than Graham's value investing system. The skill needed to be successful as a venture capitalist is rare, as evidenced by the fact that the distribution of returns in venture capital is a power law. Moats that emerge from complex adaptive systems like an economy are hard to spot. This is because a moat is something that is greater than the sum of its parts, emerging from something else that is greater than the sum of its parts. In contrast, a moat being destroyed is easier to spot because this is a process of something transforming into nothing.

Each of these three business skills is very different, and it is very unusual for a person to have all three skills. For society, this overconfidence is valuable because "even a blind squirrel finds a nut once in a while" via luck. However, at the individual level, there are a lot of unnecessary bankruptcies. What is good overall for society is not good for individuals.

VALUE INVESTING VS. FACTOR INVESTING

BEN GRAHAM AND his disciples, like Warren Buffett, Howard Marks, and Seth Klarman, have developed a system called *value investing*. Eugene Fama and Ken French developed a completely different *factor investing* approach that identifies "value stocks." Although Ben Graham's system and Fama/French's approach share the word *value*, they are vastly and fundamentally different.

It is important to draw a clear and simple definitional distinction between value as a *statistical factor* (Fama/French) and value as *an analytical style or goal* (Ben Graham). The two methods are solving for different questions: Fama/French is solving for what creates a persistent disparity of return across large numbers of stocks, while Graham-style value investors are solving for where can one find low risk of permanent impairment of capital and a high probability of an attractive return.

As a result of the fundamental differences in investing style, value stocks as identified by Fama/French's factor investing model may not be attractive at all to a value investor, as practiced by the disciples of Ben Graham. A fund constructed using factor investing has nothing to do with Ben Graham's value investing system.

The backbone of Fama/French's top-down factors model is the assumption that markets are efficient; therefore, returns that outperform the market can only be achieved by taking on greater risk. However, when Fama/French looked at the real returns of investors, they found anomalies. Because they did not want to abandon the efficient markets hypothesis, Fama/French augmented their construct with the idea that there must be undiscovered systematic "risk factors." Fama/French are now up to five such factors, one of which is the ratio of a company's book equity (shareholders' equity) to market equity (market capitalization). Thus, "book-to-market" was christened as the "value factor."

In contrast to Fama/French's top-down approach, the Ben Graham value investing system is based on the premise that to value the stock you must value the specific business on a bottoms-up basis. The Graham value investor's goal is to estimate a company's future distributable cash flows and buy it when its share price is trading significantly lower that the intrinsic value implied by these cash flows. For example, the Graham value investor might estimate that a company's long-term cash flows will be $100 million per year and buy it because the company's enterprise value is $500 million. It does not take a rocket scientist to see that if you bought something for $500 million and it returned $100 million per year, you would be getting a fantastic return on your investment (20 percent, in this case). The Graham value investing system can outperform the market over the long term, but only if the investor can do the significant work required to implement the four Graham value investing principles: (1) value shares like a proportional interest in a business, (2) have a margin of safety when purchasing shares, (3) understand Mr. Market is bipolar rather than wise and should be your servant not your master, and (4) be rational. The fourth principle is the hardest of all for investors.

Factor investing does not involve doing any of these things. When someone uses book-to-market as a ratio to measure the inexpensiveness of a stock, he or she is effectively saying that there is no difference between a pile of cash in a bank account and an operating company.

To such a person, product, customers, production capacity, brand, and operating ability mean absolutely nothing. That's because book value in the ratio is being used as a proxy for *intrinsic value*, and book value tells you nothing about a company's earnings power.

Successful Graham value investors view the world in reverse. They are concerned with what a company's operating characteristics tell you about that company's likely future cash flows. Companies with greater future cash flows are intrinsically worth more than those with less, regardless of what the book value of the companies may be.

The bridge between book value and earnings/cash flow can be found in a company's return on equity. That is: Earnings yield = Return on equity × Book to market.

Although Fama would concede that the value of a business is its discounted future cash flows, he assumes that no one can be better than average at discerning how well a company is likely to perform in the future. The implication in Fama's framework is that you might as well assume all companies have the same return on equity. If all companies have the same return on equity, then book-to-market tells you everything you need to know about a company's value. But to the Graham value investor, it is absurd to assume that there is no basis for conservatively estimating companies' future returns on equity.

Graham value investors spend a lot of time thinking about return on equity and return on capital. These are the concepts that allow them to differentiate the earnings power of one company versus that of another. To Fama/French, value is determined strictly by a database screen that sorts based on book value and price. To a Graham value investor, value is a function of margin of safety, which can be established only by measuring market price against a range of intrinsic values, constructed through a conservative estimation of future cash flows.

Here is a simple way to think about this difference using an analogy. Suppose you want to put together a basketball team (let's call it Team A). The Fama/French approach would be to recruit 100 of the tallest males in town. This team would do better than average because there is a correlation between height and ability. In the same way, there is going to be a statistical correlation between an undervalued company (e.g., a real value investment) and a company with low book-to-market.

Another approach to building the team would be to hold tryouts and actually evaluate everyone's basketball skills (as a Ben Graham style investor might evaluate a company). Someone using this style would pick the top fifteen players for this Team B. Team B is probably going to do better than Team A by a large margin, even though Team A is better than average. In the same way, a properly constructed portfolio of value investments is going to be better (by a large margin) than a portfolio with several hundred stocks with high book-to-market.

When all is said and done, the *factor investing* approach is essentially a tweak (perhaps an enhancement) on index investing. In contrast, the goal of a Graham value investor is to achieve returns that are significantly higher than a 1 to 2 percent premium. In other words, factor investing is trying to scrape out a slight statistical edge by tweaking an index fund approach, while the Graham value investor is seeking more significant returns. The proof of each approach's success is "in the doing." Investors would benefit from reflecting on the results shared in Warren Buffett's famous essay "The Superinvestors of Graham and Doddsville" to appreciate the superior results Graham value investors have historically achieved.

Perhaps this is why many funds do their best to encourage confusion about how Graham value investing differs from factor investing. They want "value" funds that are really factor investing funds to benefit from the halo of a value investing system as successfully practiced by the "superinvestors" descended from the school of Benjamin Graham.

It is an unfortunate fact that many investors appear to assume that what Warren Buffett and other Graham value investors are doing is a form of what Fama talks about when he discusses the value factor. If more investors actually read Ben Graham's *The Intelligent Investor* and other books on Graham value investing, they would realize that the approaches are fundamentally different.

NOTES

Introduction

1. Warren Buffett, *Working Together*, 2010.
2. Warren Buffett, *Tulsa World*, 2002.
3. Warren Buffett, *The Snowball*, 2008.

1. The Basics of the Graham Value Investing System

1. Peter Bevelin, *Seeking Wisdom*, 2007.
2. Janet Lowe, *Damn Right*, 2000.
3. Outstanding Investor Digest, Berkshire Hathaway Annual Meeting, 2014.
4. Seth Klarman, *Margin of Safety*, 1991.
5. Seth Klarman, Investor Letter, 2013.
6. John Bogle, *CFA Perspectives*, 2014.
7. Mungerisms, *Blogspot*, 2005.
8. Seth Klarman, *Margin of Safety*, 1991.
9. Warren Buffet, 1993 Berkshire Shareholder Letter, 1994.
10. Bruce Greenwald, *Forbes*, 2010.

2. The Principles of the Graham Value Investing System

1. Jason Zweig, *Intelligent Investor*, 2005.
2. Benjamin Graham, *Security Analysis*, 1934.
3. Benjamin Graham, *Intelligent Investor*, 2003.
4. Seth Klarman, *Margin of Safety*, 1991.
5. John Maynard Keynes, *The General Theory of Employment, Interest, and Money*, 1997.
6. Warren Buffett, *Brevelin*, 2010.
7. Gabelli, "Value Investing," 1999.
8. Benjamin Graham, *The Intelligent Investor*, 1949.
9. Ibid.
10. Warren Buffett, *The Superinvestors of Graham and Doddsville*, 1984.
11. Benjamin Graham, *Forbes*, 1932.
12. Howard Marks, Oaktree Memo, 2012.
13. Benjamin Graham, *Security Analysis*, 1934.
14. Warren Buffet, "Buy American," 2008.
15. Warren Buffett, *Fortune*, 2001.

3. Worldly Wisdom

1. Robert Hagstrom, *Latticework*, 2000.
2. Philip Tetlock, *Long Now*, 2007.
3. Bill Gates, *Poor Charlie's Almanack*, 2005.
4. Warren Buffett, *Forbes Magazine*, 1996.
5. Farris Samarrai, "Doing Something Is Better Than Doing Nothing," 2014.
6. Warren Buffett, "Working Together," 2010.
7. Warren Buffett, 2007 Berkshire Shareholder Letter, 2008.
8. Whitney Tilson, "Notes from Berkshire Shareholders Meeting," 2005.
9. Le, Dang, "Notes from 2008 Meeting with Warren Buffett," 2008.

4. The Psychology of Human Misjudgment

1. Richard Zeckhauser, "Invest in Unknown," 2006.
2. Daniel Kahneman, *Thinking Fast and Slow*, 2011.
3. Bruce Greenwald, Interview, 2013.
4. Peter D. Kaufman, *Poor Charlie's Almanack*, 2005.
5. Martin Kronicle, Interview of Michael Mauboussin, 2010.

6. Nassim Talbe, *Antifragile*, 2012.
7. Mark Twain, Letter, 1887.
8. Robert Cialdini, *Harvard Business Review*, 2013.
9. Michael Schrage, *Strategy + Business*, 2003.
10. Daniel Kahneman, *The Standard*, 2014.
11. Daniel Kahneman, *New York Times*, 2011.
12. Dan Lovallo and Daniel Kahneman, *Harvard Business Review*, 2003.
13. Chuck Jaffe, *Marketwatch*, 2012.
14. Daniel Kahneman, Interview with *The Australian*, 2012.
15. Robert Cialdini, *Influence: The Psychology of Persuasion*, 1998.
16. Robert Cialdini, *Harvard Business Review*, 2013.
17. Tim Sullivan, *Harvard Business Review*, 2011.
18. NPR Staff, *NPR*, 2013.
19. "WESCO Annual Meeting" in "The Best of Charlie Munger," 2012.

5. The Right Stuff

1. Warren Buffett, 1991 Berkshire Shareholder Letter, 1992.
2. Robert Hagstrom, *The Warren Buffet Way*, 1997.
3. Jon Templeton, *Templeton*, 2008.
4. Warren Buffett, quoted by Sather, "Berkshire Annual Meeting Recap Part II," 2008.
5. Janet Lowe, *Damn Right*, 2000.
6. Warren Buffett, 2006 Berkshire Shareholder Letter, 2007.
7. Seth Klarman, *Margin of Safety*, 1991.
8. Benjamin Franklin, *Poor Richard's Almanack*, 1732.
9. Ibid, *The Way to Wealth*, 1732.

6. The Seven Variables in the Graham Value Investing System

1. Warren Buffett, 1994 Berkshire Shareholder Letter, 1995.
2. Michael Price, Graham and Doddsville Newsletter, 2011.
3. Fred Wilson, Le Web Conference, 2014.
4. Alice Schroeder, *The Snowball*, 2008.
5. Warren Buffet, 1999 Berkshire Shareholder Letter, 2000.
6. Jason Zweig, "More Stocks May Not Make a Portfolio Safer," 2009.
7. Nassim Taleb, *Antifragile*. 2012.
8. Warren Buffett, 2012 Berkshire Shareholder Letter, 2013.

7. The Right Stuff in a Business

1. Warren Buffett, 1995 Berkshire Shareholder Letter, 1996.
2. Alice Schroeder, *The Snowball*, 2008.
3. Nassim Taleb, Paper, 2013.
4. Warren Buffet, "An Owner's Manual," 1999.
5. Michael Porter, *Competitive Strategy*, 1998.

Calculating Intrinsic Value

1. Warren Buffett, quoted in Tilson, Notes from the Berkshire Annual Meeting, 2003.

Moats

1. Warren Buffett, *Fortune*, 2012.
2. Michael Mauboussin, "Measuring the Moat," 2013.
3. Gregory Warren, "Berkshire Hathaway Retains Strong Competitive Advantage," 2014.
4. Janet Lowe, *Damn Right*, 2002.
5. Warren Buffett, quoted by Merced, Berkshire Shareholder Meeting, 2014.
6. Warren Buffett, quoted by Bossert, Berkshire Annual Meeting, 2014.
7. Ben Carlson, *A Wealth of Common Sense*, 2014.
8. Howard Marks, *The Most Important Thing*, 2011.
9. Warren Buffett, quoted in *Warren Buffet Speaks*, Janet Lowe, 2007.
10. Joseph Schumpeter, *Capitalism, Socialism, and Democracy*, 1942.
11. Michael Mauboussin, *The Blog of Michael Covel*, 1997.

GLOSSARY

ABSOLUTE FINANCIAL PERFORMANCE: the measurement of financial return against a benchmark, like a U.S. Treasury bond.

ACTIVE INVESTOR: someone picking stocks and other securities based on research, analysis, and their own judgment, rather than buying index funds and exchange-traded funds.

ALPHA: a measure of an investment's performance in relation to a benchmark, like an index.

ARBITRAGE: taking advantage of a price difference between two or more markets.

ASSET: something that has value.

ASSET CLASS: A group of assets that exhibit similar characteristics in the market (e.g., equities, bonds, and cash equivalents).

BALANCE SHEET: a financial statement that identifies a company's assets, liabilities, and shareholders' equity.

BERKSHIRE SYSTEM: an investing system that implements choices made by Munger and Buffett about variables that supplement Graham value investing.

BETA: a measure of an asset's volatility in relation to the market.

BOOK VALUE: the value of total assets less the value of total liabilities.

BOOK-TO-MARKET: compares a company's book value to its share price; book equity (shareholders' equity) to market equity (market capitalization).

BOTTOM-UP: taking fundamental/micro data and building it up, trying to understand more macro phenomena.

CIGAR-BUTT STOCK: a stock bought at a sufficiently low price that you should be able to sell it at a decent profit, even though the long-term performance of the business is terrible. The cigar-butt metaphor comes from the idea that the stock can be bought and the value comes from the fact that there are still a few puffs left in it.

CIRCLE OF COMPETENCE: the perimeter of the area within which a person has superior knowledge and expertise over the market.

CONSUMER SURPLUS: the difference between what a consumer was willing to pay and what they actually pay.

CONTRARIAN INVESTING: investing in companies that most other investors believe will not increase in value (i.e., not following the crowd).

CORRELATION: how asset prices move in relation to each other.

DEPRECIATION: an accounting allocation of the cost of a long-lived asset over its useful life.

DERIVATIVES: securities that derive their value from other securities.

DISCOUNTED CASH FLOW (DCF): discounting at an appropriate interest rate the net cash flows from an investment.

DIVERSIFICATION: buying a number of different uncorrelated assets.

DOWNSIDE: a potential loss.

EARNINGS PER SHARE (EPS): measure of profitability calculated by dividing net income by the number of shares of stock.

EBIT: earnings before interest and taxes.

EBITDA: earnings before interest, taxes, depreciation, and amortization; Munger suggests inserting the words "bullshit earnings" instead when the term is seen.

ECONOMIES OF SCALE: average costs decrease as output increases.

EFFICIENT MARKET HYPOTHESIS: at any given time, security prices fully reflect all available information (weak, semi-strong, and strong variants exist).

EQUITY: a share of company ownership.

EXTRAPOLATION: making predictions about the future based on trends from the past plus present data.

FACTOR INVESTING: an approach to investing developed by Fama/French, which has identified factors that can be used to improve index funds.

FOCUS INVESTING: an approach to investing that "implies 10 holdings, not 100 or 400," according to Munger.

FREE CASH FLOW: cash available after expenses, debt service, capital expenditures, and dividends are taken into account.

FUNDAMENTAL ANALYSIS: an analysis of performance data reported by the company itself in documents like annual reports, earnings announcements, and U.S. Securities and Exchange Commission filings.

GAAP: generally accepted accounting principles.

GRAHAM VALUE INVESTING: a type of value investing based on four fundamental principles.

GROWTH STOCK: according to Howard Marks, these are stocks (even those whose current value is low relative to their current price) with values that investors believe will grow quickly enough in the future to produce substantial appreciation.

HEDGE: the purchase of an asset intended to deliver an inverse return to another asset to offset the impact of price changes.

HEURISTICS: a mental shortcut that enables people to solve problems and make judgments quickly (mental rules of thumb).

HOLDUP PROBLEM: when an exclusive supplier (or buyer) uses that relationship to raise prices and extract profits from the buyer (or seller).

INCOME STATEMENT: a document identifying the profit or loss of a company.

INDEX INVESTOR: investing in a diversified portfolio of index funds and exchange-traded funds.

INTRINSIC VALUE: the present value of future cash flows.

INVESTMENT: the purchase of an asset in order to generate a return.

INVESTOR: someone trying to understand the underlying value of an asset.

LATTICEWORK OF MODELS: assembling many big models from many disciplines into an interrelated structure that resembles a lattice to make better decisions.

LEVERAGE: debt or borrowing as a share of a company's total funding.

LIQUIDATION VALUE: the amount of cash and assets that could be obtained breaking up the company, selling its assets, repaying its debt, and distributing everything that remains to shareholders.

LIQUIDITY: a measure of how easy it is to sell an asset for cash.

LONG: To buy something based on a prediction its price will go up.

MACROECONOMICS: the study of the aggregate behavior of an economy.

MARGIN OF SAFETY: the difference between the intrinsic value and the current market price.

MENTAL MODELS: working cognitive representations of phenomena with which people interact.

MICROECONOMICS: the study of individual elements that make up an economy.

MOAT: barriers to market entry that enable sustainable value creation by a business.

MOMENTUM INVESTING: investing based on a thesis that perceived trends in a variable, like prices, are more likely to continue than change direction.

MR. MARKET: a metaphor for the unpredictably bipolar nature of markets in the short term; sometimes in the short term, it will sell an asset at a bargain price and sometimes pay more than the asset is worth.

NET-NET STOCK: shares of stock that are traded at a discount to liquidation value.

NET PRESENT VALUE: the present value of the cash flows from the investment less the cost of the investment.

NETWORK EFFECTS: demand-side economies of scale.

OPPORTUNITY COST: the value of the foregone alternative.

OWNER'S EARNINGS: net income + depreciation + depletion + amortization − capital expenditure − additional working capital.

PASSIVE INVESTOR: investing in a diversified portfolio of index funds and exchange-traded funds.

PRESENT VALUE: amount of cash today that is equivalent in value to a payment(s) that will be received in the future.

PRIVATE MARKET VALUE: the price that a well-informed and experienced businessperson would pay for a business in a private transaction.

PRODUCER SURPLUS: difference between the amount a producer of a good or service is paid and the costs to supply that good or service.

REAL RETURN: investment return after being adjusted for the impact of inflation.

RELATIVE RETURN: the financial return when compared to a benchmark over a period of time.

RETURN ON CAPITAL: measures the return earned on capital invested in an investment.

RETURN ON EQUITY: net income generated as a percentage of shareholders' equity.

REVERSION TO THE MEAN: the tendency for later observations of random variables to be closer to their mean than current observations.

RISK: the possibility of suffering a loss.

SECURITY: debt or equity instrument issued by a private firm or government.

SHORT: the sale of a borrowed security based on a prediction that the price will drop.

SPECULATOR: someone trying to guess the price of an asset in the future by guessing what the behavior of others will be in the future.

TECHNICAL ANALYSIS: analyzing prices by using market-generated data, such as earnings ratios, volatility, price history, price patterns, and trading volume in order to time the direction of markets.

TOP-DOWN: taking big picture data and trying to use that data to understand more micro fundamentals and to choose specific investments.

TREASURY BILLS: obligations of the U.S. government sold at a discount to face value with a term of one year or less.

TREASURY BONDS: obligations of the U.S. government with a term of ten years or more, which pay interest on the principal amount.

TREASURY NOTES: obligations of the U.S. government with a term of one to ten years, which pay interest on the principal amount.

TREASURY YIELD: the percentage return on investment on the debt obligations of the U.S. government.

UPSIDE: a potential gain.

VALUE: the worth of something calculated by using fundamental analysis.

VALUE INVESTING: acquiring more than you are paying for (common to all intelligent investing).

VALUE STOCK: a term different people with different investment styles use for different purposes; factor investors have one definition and Graham value investors have another definition.

VOLATILITY: fluctuation of a variable such as a market price over time.

WORLDLY WISDOM: the routine use via synthesis of the big ideas in each of the big disciplines in making decisions.

YIELD: the income earned on an investment or a specific period.

BIBLIOGRAPHY

Video Sources

"21st Annual Conference: Roundtable III." YouTube video, 1:11:36, from a panel discussion on China at the 21st Annual Conference, posted by "committee100," June 3, 2013, http://www.youtube.com/watch?v=cDDPtJzGyEg.

"A Conversation with Charlie Munger U Michigan 2010 part 9." YouTube video, 10:24, from a talk at University of Michigan in 2010, posted by "investingtipsadvice," July 13, 2012, http://www.youtube.com/watch?v=u1RNpToWVpQ.

"Charlie Munger on BYD." YouTube video, 8:02, from an interview on Fox Television, posted by "Value Investing Pro," May 19, 2009, http://www.youtube.com/watch?v=rZ9A0oeFe9E.

"Charlie Munger Reveals Secrets to Getting Rich." YouTube video, 10:56, from a BBC interview, posted by "CharlieMungerChannel," July 13, 2012, http://www.youtube.com/watch?v=3WkpQ4PpId4.

"Charlie Munger Speech at USC—May 2007 (part 1 of 5)." YouTube video, 8:45, from a speech at USC Law School's Commencement in May 2007, posted by "Tri Suseno," August 9, 2009. http://www.youtube.com/watch?v=L6Cy7UwsRPQ.

"Munger on Sokol: 'I'm Sad.'" YouTube video, 6:27, from an interview with CNN, posted by "CNNMoney," May 3, 2011, http://www.youtube.com/watch?v=72t70apvbas.

"The Psychology of Human Misjudgment." YouTube video, 1:16:22, from a speech given at Harvard University in June 1995, posted by "BuffettMungerWisdom," January 13, 2013, http://www.youtube.com/watch?v=pqzcCfUglws.

Text Sources

Ablan, Jennifer and Jonathan Stempel. "Munger: Hard to Find Berkshire Deals, 'Raving Mad' Not to Try." Reuters, May 3, 2013. http://www.reuters.com/article/2013/05/03/us-berkshire-agm-munger-idUSBRE9420PM20130503.

Ariely, Dan. *Predictably Irrational: The Hidden Forces That Shape Our Decisions*. New York: Harper, 2010.

Barbosa, Miguel. "Interview with Michael Mauboussin." *Seeking Alpha*. September, 2009. http://m.seekingalpha.com/article/163743.

Berkowitz, Bruce. "Interview at University of Miami." *Market Folly*. November 30, 2012. http://www.marketfolly.com/2012/11/bruce-berkowitz-interview-at-university.html.

Bernstein, Peter. *Against the Gods: The Remarkable Story of Risk*. Hoboken, NJ: Wiley, 1998.

Bernstein, William. *The Investor's Manifesto*. New York: Wiley, 2012.

Betterment. "Why a Value Investor Is Better Off in a Portfolio." Interview of Bruce Greenwald. April 12, 2013. https://www.betterment.com/blog/2013/12/04/why-a-value-investor-is-better-off-in-a-portfolio.

Bevelin, Peter. *Seeking Wisdom: From Darwin to Munger*. Marceline, MO: Walsworth, 2008.

Bogle, John. "The Arithmetic of 'All-In' Investment Expenses. CFA Perspectives." *Financial Accountants Journal*, Vol. 70 (1), 2014. http://www.cfapubs.org/doi/sum/10.2469/faj.v70.n1.1

Bogle, John. *Clash of Cultures*. Hoboken, NJ: Wiley, 2012.

Bogle, John. *Common Sense on Mutual Funds: New Imperatives for the Intelligent Investor*. Hoboken, NJ: Wiley, 1999.

Bogle, John. *John Bogle on Investing: The First 50 Years*. New York: McGraw-Hill, 2000.

Bogle, John. *The Little Book of Common Sense Investing: The Only Way to Guarantee Your Fair Share of Stock Market Returns (Little Book Big Profits)*. Hoboken, NJ: Wiley, 2007.

Boodell, Peter. "2008 Berkshire Hathaway Shareholder Meeting." *Seeking Alpha*, May 5, 2008. http://seekingalpha.com/article/75598–2008-berkshire-hathaway-shareholder-meeting-detailed-notes.

Boodell, Peter. "Berkshire Hathaway Annual Meeting Notes." *Rational Walk*, May 3, 2010. http://www.rationalwalk.com/?p=6794.

Boodell, Peter. "Wesco 2008 Annual Meeting Notes." August 2009. http://mungerisms.blogspot.com/2009/08/2008-annual-meeting-notes.html.

Boodell, Peter. "Wesco Annual Meeting." *Seeking Alpha*, May 9, 2008. http://seekingalpha.com/article/76538–2008-wesco-shareholder-meeting-detailed-notes.

Bossert, Alex. 2014 Berkshire Hathaway Annual Meeting, 2014. http://www.scribd.com/doc/222892108/2014-Berkshire-Hathaway-Annual-Meeting#scribd.

Browne, Christopher. *The Little Book of Value Investing*. Hoboken, NJ: Wiley, 2006.

Bruck, Connie. "Rough Rider." *New Yorker*, November 12, 2007. http://www.newyorker.com/reporting/2007/11/12/071112fa_fact_bruck.

Bruni, Jerome V. "2004 Berkshire Hathaway Annual Meeting Top 20 Questions." *J.V. Bruni and Company Website*, 2004. http://jvbruni.com/berkshire.htm.

Bruni, Jerome V. "2005 Berkshire Hathaway Annual Meeting Top 20 Questions." *J.V. Bruni and Company Website*, 2005. http://www.jvbruni.com/Berkshire2005annualmeeting.htm.

Bruni, Jerome V. "2006 Berkshire Hathaway Annual Meeting Top 20 Questions." *J.V. Bruni and Company Website*, 2006. http://jvbruni.com/Berkshire2006annualmeeting.htm.

Bruni, Jerome V. "2007 Berkshire Hathaway Annual Meeting Top 20 Questions." *J.V. Bruni and Company Website*, 2007. http://www.jvbruni.com/Berkshire2007annualmeeting.htm.

Buffett, Warren. 1981 Berkshire Hathaway Shareholder Letter, February 26, 1982. http://www.berkshirehathaway.com/letters/1981.html.

Buffett, Warren. 1987 Berkshire Hathaway Shareholder Letter, February 29, 1988. http://www.berkshirehathaway.com/letters/1987.html.

Buffett, Warren. 1989 Berkshire Hathaway Shareholder Letter, March 2, 1990. http://www.berkshirehathaway.com/letters/1989.html.

Buffett, Warren. 1991 Berkshire Hathaway Shareholder Letter, February 28, 1992. http://www.berkshirehathaway.com/letters/1991.html.

Buffett, Warren. 1992 Berkshire Hathaway Shareholder Letter, March 1, 1993. http://www.berkshirehathaway.com/letters/1992.html.

Buffett, Warren. 1993 Berkshire Hathaway Shareholder Letter, March 1, 1994. http://www.berkshirehathaway.com/letters/1993.html.

Buffett, Warren. 1994 Berkshire Hathaway Shareholder Letter, March 7, 1995. http://www.berkshirehathaway.com/letters/1994.html.

Buffett, Warren. 1995 Berkshire Hathaway Shareholder Letter, March 1, 1996. http://www.berkshirehathaway.com/letters/1995.html.

Buffett, Warren. 1999 Berkshire Hathaway Shareholder Letter, March 1, 2000. http://www.berkshirehathaway.com/letters/1999htm.html.

Buffett, Warren. 2007 Berkshire Hathaway Shareholder Letter, February, 2008. http://www.berkshirehathaway.com/letters/2007ltr.pdf.

Buffett, Warren. 2012 Berkshire Hathaway Shareholder Letter, March 1, 2013. http://www.berkshirehathaway.com/letters/2012ltr.pdf.

Buffett, Warren. "Benjamin Graham 1894–1976." *Financial Analysts Journal*, November/December, 1976 Vol. 32, No. 6: 19. http://dx.doi.org/10.2469/faj.v32.n6.19.

Buffett, Warren. Berkshire Hathaway Website. www.berkshirehathaway.com.

Buffett, Warren. "Buy American. I am." *New York Times*, October 16, 2008. http://www.nytimes.com/2008/10/17/opinion/17buffett.html.

Buffett, Warren. "Investing in Equity Markets." Transcript of a seminar. Columbia University Business School, March 13, 1985.

Buffett, Warren. Letter to Partners. May 29, 1969.

Buffett, Warren. Letter to Partners. October 9, 1967.

Buffett, Warren. Letter to the Editor. *Forbes*. October 7, 1996.

Buffet, Warren. "An Owner's Manual." *Berkshire Hathaway*, January 1999. http://www.berkshirehathaway.com/owners.html.

Buffett, Warren. The Superinvestors of Graham-and-Doddsville. Transcript of a Speech Given at Columbia University, 1984.

Buffett, Warren. "What We Can Learn from Philip Fisher." *Forbes*. October 19, 1987.

Buffett, Warren, Walter Schloss, and Irving Kahn. A Tribute to Benjamin Graham. *Outstanding Investor Digest*. May 5, 1995.

Buffett, Warren Jr. [pseud]. "Berkshire Hathaway Annual Meeting Report." *The Motley Fool*, May 7, 2007. https://www.fool.com/community/pod/2007/070507.htm.

Buhayar, Noah. "Berkshire Hathaway's Charlie Munger Shows a Golden Touch." *Business Week*, July 25, 2013.

Bvalue. "Berkshire Meeting Notes." *The Motley Fool*, April 28, 2001.

Carlson, Ben. "Buffett in the Down Years." *A Wealth of Common Sense,* 2014. http://awealthofcommonsense.com/buffett-years.

Calvey, Mark. "Friendly Investment Advice from Warren Buffet's Buddy." *San Francisco Business Journal,* October 20, 1996. http://www.bizjournals.com/sanfrancisco/stories/1996/10/21/newscolumn6.html.

Carnegie, Dale. *How to Win Friends and Influence People*. New York: Pocket Books. Originally published 1937.

Chien, Yi Li. "Chasing Returns Has a High Cost for Investors." *St. Louis Fed*, April 14, 2014. http://www.stlouisfed.org/on-the-economy/chasing-returns-has-a-high-cost-for-investors.

Cialdini, Robert. *Influence: The Psychology of Persuasion*. New York: HarperCollins, 1998.

Claremon, Ben. "2009 Berkshire Hathaway Annual Meeting Notes." *The Inoculated Investor*, May 5, 2009. http://inoculatedinvestor.blogspot.com/2009/05/2009-berkshire-hathway-annual-meeting.html.

Claremon, Ben. "2010 Wesco Annual Meeting Notes." *Street Capitalist*, May 7, 2010. http://streetcapitalist.com/2010/05/07/charlie-mungers-2010-wesco-annual-meeting.

Claremon, Ben. "Berkshire Hathaway Annual Meeting Notes 2010: Thoughts from Warren Buffett & Charlie Munger." *Market Folly*, May 5, 2010. http://www.marketfolly.com/2010/05/berkshire-hathaway-annual-meeting-notes.html.

Claremon, Ben. "Comprehensive 2011 Berkshire Meeting Notes." *The Inoculated Investor*, May 2, 2011. http://inoculatedinvestor.blogspot.com/2011/05/comprehensive-2011-berkshire-meeting.html.

Claremon, Ben. "Notes from the Final Conversation with Charlie Munger." *The Inoculated Investor*, July 4, 2011. http://inoculatedinvestor.blogspot.com/2011/07/notes-from-final-conversation-with.html.

Cliffe, Sarah. "The Uses (and Abuses) of Influence." *Harvard Business Review*, July-August 2013. http://hbr.org/2013/07/the-uses-and-abuses-of-influence/ar/1

Cramden, Ralph. "Wesco AGM." *The Motley Fool*, May 6, 2010. http://boards.fool.com/wesco-agm-28494646.aspx?sort=postdate.

Crippen, Alex. "Charlie Munger Blasts Bankers and High-Frequency Trading." *CNBC* video, 37:00. May 3, 2013. http://www.cnbc.com/id/100707283.

Crippen, Alex. "CNBC: Notes from 1998 Berkshire Meeting." *Everything Warren Buffett*, May 2, 2008. http://everythingwarrenbuffett.blogspot.com/2008/05/cnbc-notes-from-1998-berkshire-meeting.html.

Crippen, Alex. "CNBC Transcript: Warren Buffett, Charlie Munger and Bill Gates," *CNBC*, May 5, 2014. http://www.cnbc.com/id/101642613.

Crippen, Alex. "Live Blog Archive: Warren Buffett News Conference." *CNBC*, May 4, 2008. http://www.cnbc.com/id/24454708.

Cunningham, Lawrence A. *The Essays of Warren Buffett: Lessons for Corporate America by Warren E. Buffett*. Durham, NC: Carolina Academic Press, 2008.

Daily Journal to Justin Dobbie, March 18, 2014. http://www.sec.gov/Archives/edgar/data/783412/000143774913003140/filename1.htm.

Dorsey, Pat. "Ideas That Will Make You Money." *Graham and Doddsville*, May 17, 2006. http://www.grahamanddoddsville.net/wordpress/Files/Gurus/Charlie%20Munger/Ideas%20That%20Will%20Make%20You%20Money%20-%20Morningstar%20-%205–17–06.pdf.

Eisner, Michael and Aaron Cohen. *Working Together: Why Great Partnerships Succeed*. New York: HarperCollins, 2010.

Ellis, Charles D. and James R. Verton. *Classics: An Investor's Anthology*. New York: Dow Jones-Irwin, 1989.

Fernandes, Daniel, John Lynch, and Richard Netemeyer. "Financial Literacy, Financial Education and Downstream Financial Behaviors." *Management Science*, January 6, 2014. http://papers.ssrn.com/sol3/papers.cfm?abstract_id=2333898#.

Finkelstein, Daniel. "Interview with Daniel Kahneman." *The Australian*, June 2012.

Fisher, Philip A. *Common Stocks and Uncommon Profits*. Hoboken, NJ: Wiley, 2001.

Fisher, Philip A. *Common Stocks and Uncommon Profits, Paths to Wealth through Common Stocks, Conservative Investors Sleep Well, and Developing an Investment Philosophy*. Hoboken, NJ: Wiley, 2012.

Franklin, Benjamin. *Poor Richards Almanack*. 1758.

Franklin, Benjamin. *The Way to Wealth*. 1758.

Funk, Josh. "Buffett's #2 Man Helps From the Background." *USA Today*, May 17, 2008. http://usatoday30.usatoday.com/money/markets/2008–05–17-berkshire-munger_N.htm.

Gabelli. "Value Investing—U.S." December 30, 1999. http://www.gabelli.com/news/articles/reg-selby_123099.html.

Gawande, Atul. *The Checklist Manifesto*. New York: Picador, 2011

Gdefelice. "WESCO Meeting Notes." *The Motley Fool*, May 9, 2002. http://boards.fool.com/wesco-meeting-notes-17195126.aspx.

Godwin, Richard. "The Thought Father: Nobel Prize-Winning Psychologist Daniel Kahneman on Luck." *The Standard*, March 18, 2014. http://www.standard.co.uk/lifestyle/london-life/the-thought-father-nobel-prizewinning-psychologist-daniel-kahneman-on-luck-9199162.html.

Gongol, Brian. "Notes from the 2012 Berkshire Hathaway Shareholder's Meeting." *Gongol.com*, May 7, 2012. http://www.gongol.com/research/berkshire/2012.

Graham, Benjamin. *The Intelligent Investor* (Revised edition). New York: Harper-Collins, 2003.

Graham, Benjamin. *The Memoirs of the Dean of Wall Street*. New York: McGraw-Hill, 1996.

Graham, Benjamin, Davis Dodd, Sidney Cottle, and Charles Tatham. *Security Analysis*. New York: McGraw-Hill, 1962.

Greenwald, Bruce C.N., Judd Kahn, Paul D. Sonkin, and Michael van Biema. *Value Investing, from Graham to Buffett and Beyond*. Hoboken, NJ: Wiley, 2001.

Grundfest, Joseph. "Interview with Charles Munger." *Manual of Ideas,* Spring 2009. http://www.manualofideas.com/files/content/200905_munger.pdf.

Grundfest, Joseph. "Interview with Charles Munger." *Stanford Lawyer*, May 14, 2009. http://www.calculatedriskblog.com/2009/05/interview-with-charlie-munger.html.

Hagstrom, Robert G. *Investing: The Last Liberal Art*. Cheshire, UK: Texere, 2000.

Hagstrom, Robert G. *Latticework: The News Investing*. Cheshire, UK: Texere, 2000.

Hagstrom, Robert G. *The Warren Buffett Portfolio: Mastering the Power of the Focused Investment Strategy.* New York: Wiley, 1999.

Hagstrom, Robert G. *The Warren Buffett Way*. New York: Wiley, 1997.

Henderson, Nicholas. "Wesco Annual Meeting—The Charlie Munger Show." *Gurufocus,* May 15, 2008. http://www.gurufocus.com/news/27308/the-wesco-annual-meeting—the-charlie-munger-show.

Housel, Morgan. "I'm Just Now Realizing How Stupid We Are." *The Motley Fool*, June 14, 2014. http://www.fool.com/investing/general/2014/06/11/im-just-now-realizing-how-stupid-we-are.aspx.

Huey, John. "The World's Best Brand." *Fortune*, May 31, 1993. http://management.fortune.cnn.com/2012/11/21/buffett-coke-brand/.

The Investments Blog. "Final Wesco Meeting: A Morning with Charlie Munger." *The Investments Blog*, July 4, 2011. http://theinvestmentsblog.blogspot.com/2011/07/final-wesco-meeting-morning-with.html.

Irwin, Neal. "After Buffett, Should Berkshire Hathaway Be Broken Up?" *New York Times*, May 5, 2014. http://www.nytimes.com/2014/05/06/upshot/should-berkshire-hathaway-be-broken-up.html.

Jaffe, Chuck. "Commentary: Superior Beliefs Bring Inferior Results." *Marketwatch*, May 18, 2012. http://www.marketwatch.com/story/how-investors-think-their-way-into-trouble-2012-05-18.

Kahn, Irving, and Robert Milne. *Benjamin Graham: The Father of Financial Analysis*. Charlottesville, VA: Financial Analysts Research Foundation, 1977.

Kahneman, Daniel. "Don't Blink! The Hazards of Confidence." *New York Times*, October 19, 2011.

Kahneman, Daniel. *Thinking, Fast and Slow*. New York: Farrar, Straus and Giroux, 2011.

Kass, David. "Notes from 2012 Berkshire Hathaway Annual Meeting." *Warren Buffett Blog, Robert H. Smith School of Business,* June 4, 2012. http://blogs.rhsmith.umd.edu/davidkass/uncategorized/notes-from-2012-berkshire-hathaway-annual-meeting.

Kass, David. "Notes from 2013 Berkshire Hathaway Annual Meeting." *Warren Buffett Blog, Robert H. Smith School of Business,* May 31, 2013. http://

blogs.rhsmith.umd.edu/davidkass/uncategorized/notes-from-2013-berkshire-hathaway-annual-meeting.

Kass, David. "Notes from Berkshire Hathaway Annual Meeting—April 30, 2011." *Warren Buffett Blog, Robert H. Smith School of Business,* June 26, 2011. http://blogs.rhsmith.umd.edu/davidkass/uncategorized/berkshire-hathaway-annual-meeting-april-30–2011.

Kass, David. "Warren Buffett's Meeting with University of Maryland MBA Students—November 15, 2013." *Warren Buffet Blog, Robert H. Smith School of Business,* December 8, 2013. http://blogs.rhsmith.umd.edu/davidkass/uncategorized/warren-buffetts-meeting-with-university-of-maryland-mbams-students-november-15–2013.

Kass, Peter. *The Book of Investing Wisdom: Classic Writings by Great Stock-Pickers and Legends of Wall Street.* New York: Wiley, 1999.

Kaufman, Peter D. *Poor Charlie's Almanack: The Wit and Wisdom of Charles T. Munger.* Virginia Beach, VA: Donning, 2005.

Kelley, Margie. "In the Money." *Harvard Law Bulletin,* Summer 2001. http://www.law.harvard.edu/news/bulletin/2001/summer/feature_1–1.html.

Keynes, John Maynard. *The General Theory of Employment, Interest, and Money.* Amherst, NY: Prometheus Books, 1997.

Klarman, Seth. *Margin of Safety.* New York: Harper, 1991.

Korada, Srinivas. "Notes from WESCO's Annual Meeting." *Gurufocus,* May 8, 2009. http://www.gurufocus.com/news/55358/notes-from-wescos-annual-meeting

Kronicle, Martin. "Think Twice Michael Mauboussin Interview." *Martinkronicle*, 2010. http://www.martinkronicle.com/2010/05/04/think-twice-michael-mauboussin-interview/.

Kupfer, Andrew. "Gates on Buffett." *Fortune*, February 6, 1996. http://money.cnn.com/magazines/fortune/fortune_archive/1996/02/05/207334/index.htm.

LaFon, Holly. "Buffett and Munger Annual Meeting 2013 Q&A." *The Motley Fool*, May 8, 2013. http://www.marketfolly.com/2013/02/notes-from-charlie-mungers-daily.html.

LaFon, Holly. "Buffett and Munger Annual Meeting 2013 Q&A." *Gurufocus,* May 8, 2013. http://www.gurufocus.com/news/218379/buffett-and-munger-annual-meeting-2013-qa-complete.

Le, Dang. "Notes from 2008 Meeting with Warren Buffett." *Underground Value*, February 23, 2008. http://undergroundvalue.blogspot.com/2008/02/notes-from-buffett-meeting-2152008_23.html.

Lefevre, Edwin. *Reminisces of a Stock Operator*. Hoboken, NJ: Wiley, 2006.

Lenzer, Robert. "The Unadulterated Wit and Wisdom of Charlie Munger." *Forbes,* May 12, 2010. http://www.forbes.com/2010/05/12/charlie-munger-warren-buffett-markets-streettalk-berkshire-hathaway.html.

Loomis, Carol. "Warren Buffett on the Stock Market." *Fortune*, December 10, 2001. http://www.tilsonfunds.com/BuffettStockMarket.pdf.

Lovallo, Dan and Daniel Kahneman. "Delusions of Success: How Optimism Undermines Executives' Decisions." *Harvard Business Review*, July 2003. https://hbr.org/2003/07/delusions-of-success-how-optimism-undermines-executives-decisions.

Lowe, Janet. *Benjamin Graham on Value Investing: Lessons from the Dean of Wall Street*. New York: Penguin, 1994.

Lowe, Janet. *Damn Right: Behind the Scenes with Berkshire Hathaway Billionaire: Charlie Munger.* Hoboken, NJ: Wiley, 2000.

Lowe, Janet. *The Rediscovered Benjamin Graham*. Hoboken, NJ: Wiley, 1999.

Lowe, Janet. *Value Investing Made Easy*. New York: McGraw-Hill, 1996.

Lowe, Janet. *Warren Buffet Speaks: Wit and Wisdom from the World's Greatest Investor*. Hoboken, NJ: Wiley, 2007.

Lowenstein, Roger. *Buffett: The Making of an American Capitalist*. New York: Random House, 1997.

Lowenstein, Roger. *When Genius Failed*. New York: Random House, 2000.

Lu, Li. "My Teacher: Charlie Munger." *China Entrepreneur*, May 21, 2010.

Lynch, Peter. *Beating the Street*. New York: Simon and Schuster, 1994.

Lynch, Peter. *On up on Wall Street*. New York: Simon and Schuster, 2000.

Mackay, Harvey. "The Oracle of Omaha Speaks." *Tulsa World*, July 7, 2002.

Mackintosh, James. "FT Long Short." *Financial Times*, February 14, 2013. http://blogs.ft.com/ft-long-short/2013/02/14/be-like-buffett.

Majmudar, Kaushal B. "Warren Buffett's Wisdom on Investing, on Markets, and on Life." *Gurufocus*, May 21, 2006. http://www.gurufocus.com/news/1636/warren-buffetts-wisdom-on-investing-on-markets-and-on-life.

Malkiel, Burton. *A Random Walk Down Wall Street*. New York: W.W. Norton, 1985.

Mandelbrot, Benoit. *The Misbehavior of Markets*. New York: Basic Books, 2004.

Maranjian, Selena. "Berkshire Hathaway Annual Meeting Notes." *The Motley Fool*, May 7, 2002. http://boards.fool.com/press-conference-part-1–12517974.aspx.

Maranjian, Selena. "Berkshire Hathaway Press Conference Notes." *The Motley Fool*, May 7, 2002. http://boards.fool.com/berkshire-hathaway-press-conference-notes-17180279.aspx 2002.

Maranjian, Selena. "Berkshire Hathaway's Other Half." *The Motley Fool*, January 9, 2001. http://www.fool.com/specials/2001/sp010109.htm.

Maranjian, Selena. "Press Conference." *The Motley Fool*, May 4, 2000. http://boards.fool.com/press-conference-part-1–12517974.aspx.

Marks, Howard. Oaktree Capital Memo. Oaktree Capital Management, June 20, 2012.

Marks, Howard. Oaktree Capital Memo. Oaktree Capital Management, July 16, 2014.

Marks, Howard. *The Most Important Thing: Uncommon Sense for the Thoughtful Investor.* New York: Columbia Business School Publishing, 2011.

Martin, Michael. "Think Twice." Michael Mauboussin Interview, May 4, 2010. http://www.martinkronicle.com/2010/05/04/think-twice-michael-mauboussin-interview.

Mauboussin, Michael. "Are You an Expert?" *The Blog of Michael Covel.* October 28, 2005. www.capatcolumbia.com/ . . . /Are%20You%20an%20Expert.pdf.

Mauboussin, Michael. "Aver and Aversion." *The Blog of Michael Covel.* January 6, 2006. http://www.michaelcovel.com/2006/01/06/aver-and-aversion.

Mauboussin, Michael. "The Babe Ruth Effect." *The Consilient Observer*, 2002. http://turtletrader.com/pdfs/babe-ruth.pdf.

Mauboussin, Michael. "Big Think Interview with Michael Mauboussin." May 14, 2010. http://bigthink.com/videos/big-think-interview-with-michael-mauboussin.

Mauboussin, Michael. "Blaming the Rat." *The Blog of Michael Covel,* 2011. http://michaelcovel.com/pdfs/BlamingtheRat.pdf.

Mauboussin, Michael. "Capital Ideas Revisited." *The Blog of Michael Covel,* March 30, 2005. http://turtletrader.com/pdfs/CapitalIdeasRevisited03_30_05.pdf.

Mauboussin, Michael. "Embracing Complexity." *Harvard Business Review*, September 2011. http://hbr.org/2011/09/embracing-complexity/ar/1.

Mauboussin, Michael. "Explaining the Wisdom of Crowds." *The Blog of Michael Covel,* 2007. http://www.capatcolumbia.com/Articles/ExplainingtheWisdomofCrowds.pdf.

Mauboussin, Michael. "Frontiers of Finance." *The Blog of Michael Covel,* 1997. http://people.stern.nyu.edu/adamodar/pdfiles/eqnotes/cap.pdf.

Mauboussin, Michael. "Frontiers of Strategy." *The Blog of Michael Covel,* 1998. http://www.capatcolumbia.com/Articles/FoStrategy/Fos1.pdf.

Mauboussin, Michael. "Get Real." *The Blog of Michael Covel,* 1999. http://www.capatcolumbia.com/Articles/FoFinance/Fof10.pdf.

Mauboussin, Michael. "An Interview with Behavioral Investing Expert Michael Mauboussin." Matt Koppenheffer, March 1, 2014. http://www.fool.com/investing/general/2014/03/01/an-interview-with-behavioral-investing-expertmich.aspx.

Mauboussin, Michael. "Interview with Michael Mauboussin." Big Think. http://bigthink.com/videos/big-think-interview-with-michael-mauboussin (no date given, but "over four years ago").

Mauboussin, Michael. "Is Your Manager Skillful or Just Lucky?" *Wall Street Journal,* November 2, 2012. http://online.wsj.com/news/articles/SB10000872396390444734804578062890110146284.

Mauboussin, Michael. "Measuring the Moat: Assessing the Magnitude and Sustainability of Value Creation." *Credit Suisse*, December 16, 2002. http://www.safalniveshak.com/wp-content/uploads/2012/07/Measuring-The-Moat-CSFB.pdf.

Mauboussin, Michael. "Michael Mauboussin on the Santa Fe Institute and Complex Adaptive Systems." *Compounding My Interests Blog*, November 7, 2013. http://compoundingmyinterests.com/compounding-the-blog/2013/11/7/michael-mauboussin-on-the-santa-fe-institute-and-complex-ada.html.

Mauboussin, Michael. "Steve Forbes Interview: Michael Mauboussin, Professor and Investor." *Forbes*, July 11, 2011. http://www.forbes.com/sites/steveforbes/2011/07/11/steve-forbes-interview-michael-mauboussin-professor-and-investor/.

Mauboussin, Michael. "Valuation." 2002. http://www.capatcolumbia.com/Articles/Valuation%20-%20Mauboussin.pdf.

Mauboussin, Michael. "Mauboussin on the 'Success Equation.'" *Knowledge@Wharton*, March 6, 2013. http://knowledge.wharton.upenn.edu/article/michael-mauboussin-on-the-success-equation.

Mauboussin, Michael. *More Than You Know: Finding Financial Wisdom in Unconventional Places*. New York: Columbia University Press, 2006.

Mauboussin, Michael. *The Success Equation*. Cambridge, MA: Harvard Business Review Press, 2012.

Mauboussin, Michael. *Think Twice*. Cambridge, MA: Harvard Business Press, 2009.

Mauboussin, Michael. "Untangling Skill and Luck." *Harvard Business Review*. February 7, 2011. http://blogs.hbr.org/2011/02/untangling-skill-and-luck.

Mauboussin, Michael, and Paul Johnson. "Competitive Advantage Period 'CAP': The Neglected Value Driver." January 14, 1997. http://people.stern.nyu.edu/adamodar/pdfiles/eqnotes/cap.pdf.

Merced, Michael J. "Berkshire Hathaway's 2014 Shareholder Meeting." *New York Times*, May 3, 2014. http://dealbook.nytimes.com/2014/05/03/live-blog-berkshire-hathaways-2014-shareholder-meeting/?_r=2.

Montgomery, Cynthia and Michael Porter. *Strategy: Seeking and Securing Competitive Advantage*. Cambridge, MA: Harvard Business Press, 1979.

Montier, James. *Darwin's Mind: The Evolutionary Foundations of Heuristics and Biases*. Rochester, NY: Social Science Research Network, 2002.

Montier, James. "The Golden Rules of Investing." *GMO Letter*, December 2013.

Montier, James. "Only White Swans on the Way to Revulsion." *Q Finance*, November 2009. http://www.qfinance.com/capital-markets-viewpoints/only-white-swans-on-the-road-to-revulsion.

Montier, James. "The Seven Immutable Laws of Investing." *The Big Picture* 2011. http://www.ritholtz.com/blog/2011/03/the-seven-immutable-laws-of-investing/.

Munger, Charles. "Academic Economics: Strengths and Faults after Considering Interdisciplinary Needs." Speech, University of California, Santa Barbara, October 3, 2003. http://www.rbcpa.com/Munger_UCSBspeech.pdf.

Munger, Charles. Charles Munger Resignation letter from the U.S. League of Savings Institution, May 30, 1989. http://boards.fool.com/charlie-munger-long-13640415.aspx.

Munger, Charles. "Commencement Speech at Harvard School." Speech, Boston, MA, June 13, 1986. http://biznewz.com/charlie-mungers-speech-to-the-harvard-school-june-1986.

Munger, Charles. "Dubridge Lecture." Speech, California Institute of Technology, March 2008. http://www.voicebase.com/voice_file/public_detail/235138.

Munger, Charles. "How We Can Restore Market Confidence." *Washington Post,* November 2, 2009. http://articles.washingtonpost.com/2009–02–11/opinions/36831107_1_booms-investment-banks-financial-system.

Munger, Charles. "Investment Practices of Leading Charitable Foundations. Foundation Financial Officers Group." Speech, Santa Monica, CA, October 14, 1998. http://www.tiffeducationfoundation.org/SRIdocuments/Charlie_Munger_on_Institutional_Funds_Management.pdf.

Munger, Charles. "A Lesson on Elementary, Worldly Wisdom as It Relates to Investment Management & Business." Speech, University of Southern California Marshall School of Business, April 14, 1994. http://old.ycombinator.com/munger.html.

Munger, Charles. "A Lesson in Elementary, Worldly Wisdom, Revisited." Speech, Stanford Law School, April 19, 1996. http://www.scribd.com/doc/86728974/3-Lesson-in-Elementary-Worldy-Wisdom-Revisited-1996.

Munger, Charles. "Master's Class." *Philanthropy,* March/April 1999. http://www.philanthropyroundtable.org/topic/excellence_in_philanthropy/masters_class.

Munger, Charles. "Optimism Has No Place in Accounting." *Washington Post,* April 4, 2002.

Munger, Charles. "Outstanding Investor Digest." Speech, Stanford Law School Class of William Lazier, March 13, 1998.

Munger, Charles. Speech, Harvard Westlake School, January 19, 2010. http://www.valueinvestingworld.com/2012/10/santangels-review-transcript-of-charlie.html.

Munger, Charles. "Talk of Charles Munger to the Breakfast Meeting of the Philanthropy Roundtable." Washington, DC, November 10, 2000. http://mungerisms.blogspot.com/2009/09/philanthropy-round-table.html.

Munger, Charles. "The Great Financial Scandal of 2003." Speech, Wesco Financial Corporation 2001 Annual Meeting, 2001. http://www.bluechipinvestorfund.com/munger.html.

Munger, Charles. "Thought about Practical Thought." Informal talk, July 20, 1996. http://www.scribd.com/doc/76174254/Munger-s-Analysis-to-Build-a-Trillion-Dollar-Business-From-Scratch.

Munger, Charles. "Wantmore, Tweakmore, Totalscum, and the Tragedy of Boneheadia." *Slate,* July 6, 2011. http://www.slate.com/articles/business/moneybox/2011/07/wantmore_tweakmore_totalscum_and_the_tragedy_of_boneheadia.html.

Mungerian. "2006 Wesco Meeting Notes." *The Motley Fool*, May 11, 2006. http://boards.fool.com/2006-wesco-meeting-notes-long-rough-24092970.aspx.

Mungerisms. "Westco 1999 Annual Meeting" *Blogspot*, 1999. http://mungerisms.blogspot.com/2009/08/wesco-1999-annual-meeting.html.

Mungerisms. "Munger Speaks with Kiplinger's Steven Goldberg." *Blogspot*, 2005. http://mungerisms.blogspot.com/2009/09/munger-speaks-with-kiplingers-steven.html.

Neuroberk. "Westco Meeting." *The Motley Fool*, May 7, 2000. http://boards.fool.com/here-are-neuroberks-notes-from-the-wesco-12529644.aspx.

NPR Staff. "Taking a Closer Look at Milgram's Shocking Obedience Study." *NPR*, August 28, 2013. http://www.npr.org/2013/08/28/209559002/taking-a-closer-look-at-milgrams-shocking-obedience-study.

Pabrai, Mohnish. *The Dhandho Investor.* New York: Wiley, 2007.

Paladinvest. "Wesco Meeting." *The Motley Fool*, May 7, 2000. http://boards.fool.com/wesco-meeting-12529248.aspx.

Parrish, Shane. "Michael Mauboussin Interview." *Farnam Street Blog,* August 28, 2013. http://www.farnamstreetblog.com/2013/08/michael-mauboussin-interview-no-4.

Patterson, Scott. "Here's the Story on Berkshire's Munger." *Wall Street Journal,* May 1, 2009. http://online.wsj.com/news/articles/SB124113732066375503#.

Pauls, Matt. "Notes from Berkshire Hathaway's Annual Meeting, 2009." *Gurufocus,* May 6, 2009. http://www.gurufocus.com/news/54571/notes-from-berkshire-hathaways-annual-meeting-2009.

Pender, Kathleen. "Dueling Views of Reform." *SF Gate,* June 22, 2004. http://www.sfgate.com/business/networth/article/Dueling-views-of-reform-2747436.php.

Porter, Michael. *Competitive Advantage: Creating and Sustaining Superior Performance.* New York: Free Press, 1998.

Porter, Michael. "The Five Competitive Forces That Shape Strategy." *Harvard Business Review,* January 2008.

Rappaport, Alfred, and Michael Mauboussin *Expectations Investing, Reading Stock Prices for Better Returns.* Cambridge, MA: Harvard Business School Press, 2001.

Raza, Sheeraz. "Berkshire Hathaway Annual Meeting 2012." *Scribd*, May 5, 2012. http://www.scribd.com/doc/92763946/Berkshire-Hathaway-Annual-Meeting-2012.

Report on Berkshire Hathaway Annual Meeting, *Outstanding Investor Digest*, 1997.

Report on Berkshire Hathaway Annual Meeting, *Outstanding Investor Digest*, December 31, 2014.

Richards, Carl. "Indexing Is No Panacea for Investors." January 17, 2014. http://abnormalreturns.com/indexing-is-no-panacea-for-investor.

Ritholtz, Barry. "The Average Investor Needs Some Help." *Bloomberg View*, April 9, 2014. http://www.bloombergview.com/articles/2014-04-09/the-average-investor-needs-some-help-ritholtz-chart.

Roughly Right. "2003 Wesco Annual Meeting Notes." *The Motley Fool*, May 8, 2003. http://boards.fool.com/2003-wesco-annual-meeting-notes-19016644.aspx.

Roughly Right. "Berkshire Meeting Notes." *The Motley Fool*, May 4, 2002. http://boards.fool.com/2003-wesco-annual-meeting-notes-19016644.aspx.

Samarrai, Farris. "Doing Something Is Better Than Doing Nothing for Most People, Study Shows." *UVA Today*, July 3, 2014. https://news.virginia.edu/content/doing-something-better-doing-nothing-most-people-study-shows.

Sather, Dave. "Berkshire Hathaway Annual Meeting Recap Part II." *Sather Financial*, May 31, 2008. http://www.satherfinancial.com/index.php/commentaries/8/17-may2008-commentary-2.

Savitz, Eric. "The Wit and Wisdom of Charlie Munger." *Tech Trader Daily, Barron's*, June 26, 2006. http://blogs.barrons.com/techtraderdaily/2006/06/26/the-wit-and-wisdom-of-charlie-munger.

Schrage, Michael. "Daniel Kahneman: The Thought Leader Interview." *Strategy + Business*, Winter 2003. http://www.strategy-business.com/article/03409.

Schroeder, Alice. *The Snowball: Warren Buffett and the Business of Life*. New York: Random House, 2008.

Sellers, Patricia. "Warren Buffett and Charlie Munger's Best Advice." *Fortune*, October 31, 2013. http://postcards.blogs.fortune.cnn.com/2013/10/31/buffett-munger-best-advice.

Serwer, Andy. "Buffett's Alter Ego." *Fortune*, May 2, 2006. http://money.cnn.com/magazines/fortune/fortune_archive/2006/05/29/8378052/index.htm.

Simon, Herbert. "How Managers Express Their Creativity." *The McKinsey Quarterly*, Autumn 1986.

Simpleinvestor. "Free Investment Seminar." *The Motley Fool*, May 25, 1999. http://boards.fool.com/Message.asp?mid=10893331.

Smith, Adam. "Supermoney." New York: Random House, 1972.

Soros, George. *The Alchemy of Finance*. New York: Simon and Schuster, 1987.

Sullivan, Tim. “Embracing Complexity.” Interview with Michael J. Mauboussin, *Harvard Business Review,* September 2011. http://hbr.org/2011/09/embracing-complexity/ar/1.

Taleb, Nassim. *Antifragile*. New York: Random House, 2012.

Taleb, Nassim. *The Black Swan*. New York: Random House, 2007.

Taleb, Nassim. *Fooled by Randomness: The Hidden Role of Change in the Markets and in Life*. Cheshire, UK: Texere, 2001.

Taleb, Nassim. *How to Prevent Other Financial Crises*. Rochester, NY: Social Science Research Network, 2012. http://papers.ssrn.com/sol3/papers.cfm?abstract_id=2029092.

Taleb, Nassim. “The Skin in the Game Heuristic for Protection against Tail Events.” *Nassim Taleb Website*, 2013. http://nassimtaleb.org/category/skin-in-the-game.

Teabone. “Wesco Meeting Notes.” *The Motley Fool*, May 5, 2005. http://boards.fool.com/wesco-meeting-notes-22447816.aspx.

Templeton, Lauren, and Scott Phillips. *Investing the Templeton Way*. New York: McGraw Hill, 2008.

Tetlock, Philip. *Why Foxes Are Better Forecasters Than Hedgehogs*. San Francisco: Long Now Foundation, 2007.

Thaler, Richard. “What Scientific Idea Is Ready for Retirement?” *Edge*, 2014. http://www.edge.org/response-detail/25293.

Tilson, Whitney. “2006 Wesco Annual Meeting Notes.” *Whitney Tilson’s Value Investing Website,* May 11, 2006. http://www.tilsonfunds.com/wscmtg06notes.pdf.

Tilson, Whitney. “The Best of Charlie Munger.” *The Motley Fool*, May 15, 2002. http://www.fool.com/news/foth/2002/foth020515.htm.

Tilson, Whitney. “Buffett’s Wit and Wisdom.” *The Motley Fool,* May 3, 2004. http://www.fool.com/investing/general/2004/05/03/buffetts-wit-and-wisdom.asp

Tilson, Whitney. “Charlie Munger Holds Court.” *The Motley Fool,* May 8, 2001. http://www.fool.com/news/foth/2001/foth010508.htm.

Tilson, Whitney. “Charlie Munger in Rare Form.” *The Motley Fool,* May 7, 2004. http://www.fool.com/server/printarticle.aspx?file=/investing/general/2004/05/07/charlie-munger-in-rare-form.aspx.

Tilson, Whitney. “Charlie Munger Speaks: Notes from the Wesco Annual Meeting.” *The Motley Fool*, May 15, 2000. http://www.fool.com/boringport/2000/boringport000515oo.htm.

Tilson, Whitney. “Charlie Munger’s Worldly Wisdom.” *The Motley Fool,* May 5, 2003. http://www.fool.com/news/2003/05/09/charlie-mungers-worldly-wisdom.aspx.

Tilson, Whitney. "Highlights from Berkshire's Meeting." *The Motley Fool*, May 8, 2002. http://www.fool.com/news/foth/2002/foth020508.htm.

Tilson, Whitney. "Munger Goes Mental." *The Motley Fool*, June 4, 2004. http://www.fool.com/investing/general/2004/06/04/munger-goes-mental.aspx.

Tilson, Whitney. "Notes from the 2001 Wesco Annual Meeting." *Whitney Tilson's Value Investing Website*, April 28, 2001. http://www.tilsonfunds.com/motley_berkshire_wscmtg01notes.php.

Tilson, Whitney. "Notes from the 2003 Berkshire Hathaway Annual Meeting." *Whitney Tilson's Value Investing Website*, May 3, 2003. http://www.tilsonfunds.com/motley_berkshire_brkmtg03notes.php.

Tilson, Whitney. "Notes from the 2005 Berkshire Hathaway Annual Meeting." *Whitney Tilson's Value Investing Website*, April 30, 2005. http://www.tilsonfunds.com/brkmtg05notes.pdf.

Tilson, Whitney. "Notes from the 2003 Wesco Annual Meeting." *Whitney Tilson's Value Investing Website*, May 7, 2003. http://www.tilsonfunds.com/motley_berkshire_wscmtg01notes.php.

Tilson, Whitney. "Notes from the 2005 Wesco Annual Meeting." *Whitney Tilson's Value Investing Website*, May 4, 2005. www.tilsonfunds.com/wscmtg05notes.pdf.

Tilson, Whitney. "Notes from the Berkshire Hathaway Annual Meeting." *The Motley Fool*, May 1, 2000.

Train, John. *The Midas Touch*. New York: Harper & Row, 1987.

Train, John. *The Money Masters*. New York: HarperCollins, 1980.

Twain, Mark. "Letter to Mrs. Foote." December 2, 1887.

Warren, Gregory. "Berkshire Hathaway Retains Strong Competitive Advantage." *Morningstar*, April 30, 2014. http://www.morningstar.co.uk/uk/news/124079/berkshire-hathaway-retains-strong-competitive-advantage.aspx.

"WESCO Annual Meeting May 2009." In "The Best of Charlie Munger: 1994–2011. A Collection of Speeches, Essays, and Wesco Annual Meeting Notes." (unpublished manuscript, 2012), comp. Bledsoe, Yanan Ma. http://www.valueplays.net/wp-content/uploads/The-Best-of-Charlie-Munger-1994-2011.pdf.

Whitman, Martin J. *Value Investing: A Balanced Approach*. New York: Wiley, 2000.

Williams, John Burr. *The Theory of Investment Value*. Flint Hill, VA: Fraser Publishing, 1997.

Zeckhauser, Richard. "Investing in the Unknown and Unknowable." Rochester, NY: Social Science Research Network, 2006. http://papers.ssrn.com/sol3/papers.cfm?abstract_id=2205821.

Zweig, Jason. "Benjamin Graham: Building a Profession Classic Writings of the Father of Security Analysis." New York: McGraw-Hill, 2010.

Zweig, Jason. "A Fireside Chat with Charlie Munger." *Wall Street Journal*, September 12, 2014. http://blogs.wsj.com/moneybeat/2014/09/12/a-fireside-chat-with-charlie-munger.

Zweig, Jason. "More Stocks May Not Make a Portfolio Safer." *Wall Street Journal*, November 26, 2009. http://online.wsj.com/news/articles/SB10001424052748704533904574548003614347452.

Zweig, Jason. *The Intelligent Investor* (Revised edition). New York: Harper Business Essentials, 2006.

Zweig, Jason. "The Intelligent Investor: Saving Investors from Themselves." *Wall Street Journal*, June 28, 2013. http://blogs.wsj.com/moneybeat/2013/06/28/the-intelligent-investor-saving-investors-from-themselves.

Zweig, Jason. *The Little Book of Safe Money: How to Conquer Killer Markets, Con Artists, and Yourself.* Hoboken, NJ: Wiley, 2009.

Zweig, Jason. "The Oracle Speaks." *Fortune*, May 2, 2005. http://money.cnn.com/2005/05/01/news/fortune500/buffett_talks/index.htm.

Zweig, Jason. *Your Money and Your Brain: How the New Science of Neuroeconomics Can Help Make You Rich*. New York: Simon and Schuster, 2008.